I'm Not Waving...
I'm Drowning

I'm Not Waving...
I'm Drowning

Help for Those Who Need
HOPE AND HEALING

MAMIE
McCULLOUGH

CEDAR HILL PRESS

All Scripture references are from the New International Version unless otherwise designated.

ISBN 0-9702138-32

Cover: Richmond & Williams
Text: BookSetters

First Edition
Printed in the United States of America
1 2 3 4 5 6 7 — 06 05 04 03 02 01

This book is dedicated to special friends
>Barbara Hammond
>Grace Pilot
>Joyce Rowe
>Helen Beasley
>Thalia Hanna
>Elizabeth Jones

and to my children
>Scott and Jennifer Krupa
>Brian and Jennifer McCullough
>Matt and Patti Wyman
>David and Cindy Skelton

These friends and family members have had the continued patience, unconditional love, and have "prayed me up" many times as they encouraged me to finish this book. They have given me the emotional strength to share my heart with you, the reader.

Contents

Acknowledgments

To the Encourager Foundation—thanks to each of you who have loved, listened, encouraged, and cared enough to help me to help others. You are truly the best examples of how godly women mentor others.

To those of you who see yourselves on the pages of this book, you are truly the shining stars. We *can* make a difference in someone's life by committing to awareness and by taking action. I love you—and the best is yet to "bee."

To my capable, patient staff—a big thank-you for your input, editing, and encouragement to make this book a reality.

A Word from Mamie

My husband, Herschel, a former jet pilot instructor, tells me that on the darkest, most overcast days, one only has to go a few thousand feet straight up to be above the cloudy darkness and reach clear, sunny, bright skies.

You may be deciding at this time in your life which direction you should go to get away from the darkness of life's clouds and reach the sunlight. You can find clear skies and safety if you take action in the right direction. When you are out in an ocean swimming for instance, and you find you have gone too far from shore, you need to find the closest way back to keep from being pulled under by the current. My hope is that you can find the right direction to overcome your dark skies and that you find hope and healing somewhere in the pages of this book.

Throughout life, we all experience times when circumstances seem to overwhelm us. Perhaps you feel depressed or challenged in your job, in your marriage, or with your children. Perhaps you feel that you are drowning or going under and that no one notices your pleas for help.

Why does life seem so hopeless at times? I certainly don't have all the answers, but I know that as we grow through life, we make hard choices and have to live with the consequences. Many decisions put us far from the safety of the shore, and we do not know what is in the waters around us. I cannot keep problems and bad things from happening to you, but I *can* offer some life-rebuilding suggestions for reaching the shore when this happens.

It is important that you take action in the correct direction—toward the shore. In order to survive, you need to take right advice and listen to those who can help you—perhaps a total stranger will be the one who lifts your spirits and steers you in the right direction. My heartfelt desire is to offer you some layman's thoughts to encourage you, and to help you regain control. I'm asking you to take this belief today and realize you are cared about and loved: *I believe in you.*

This book is written from a layman's heart and is about hope and healing for those—whether single, married, old, young—who have felt they had no one to care, listen, or take up for them. My desire is to encourage you to "bee" all you can be on a daily basis. Begin today to heal and find hope, peace, and enjoyment in what God has created you to be. Every day is a new day in your journey of healing.

This book is written *for* you and *to* you so that you may have the courage to begin a journey of hope and healing and also that you may help others do the same. Perhaps one story or idea will be your tool to help loved ones, neighbors, or friends to enjoy the peace of a safe harbor. You have many people all around you who are waving for help because of their situations.

Who is your neighbor? Those whom you pass in your daily life at school, at the grocery store, and yes, at church—those who need your help of love and concern and even encouragement to lead them to safety. You have the ability to throw out a life jacket, and my goal is to inspire you to action.

This book is my heart for those who need encouragement; I want to talk to you as if you were sitting at my table drinking a cup of coffee with me. My goal is to give you the resources that you need to begin your journey of healing. I offer you advice, encouragement, thoughts, stories, and information—all collected by trials and error, and by lots of prayer. When our visit comes to an end, take this study guide with you as you continue your journey. As you begin, read with an open heart and mind for yourself.

Chapter 1

Waving for Help

I hope that during your childhood, you had a grandmother, an aunt, a close friend, or a mother like mine. Someone who would sit in a rocker and pull you onto her lap and hold you. There was no safer place for me than sitting on the porch in Mama's lap, smelling her fresh-starched dress and the fresh-cut grass—and listening to the whippoorwill's chant. Even as I write these words, I am there.

Someone asked me what my objective was in writing this book, what I wanted to accomplish. Simply stated, I would like to take everyone who has been hurt or abused, pull them into the safety of my lap, and hold her as she smells the fresh-starched dress and the fresh-cut grass—and listens to the whippoorwill's chant. Now, before you dismiss my desire as too simplistic, let me assure you that the experience of that scene has deep psychological ramifications. Here is just one example: Everyone needs a "safe place"—somewhere to go for comfort, peace, healing, and love. The healing process involves finding one's personal safe and accepted place.

As I head past my fifth decade, I crawl up on Mama's lap in my mind, allowing her to comfort that little girl who so desperately needed the love, attention, and kindness of a warm, unconditional,

If only I had
known
to ask for help

loving touch, who needed an arm around the shoulders. In many ways, that little girl—Mamie Claire Darlington of Dixie, Georgia—never got to be a child.

———

My daddy died when I was three years old, leaving my mama with nine kids under the age of seventeen. My father had been a share-cropper, and after his death we were left with no home. Mama could not read or write, and we had to live on welfare supplemented by work from folks around us. In southern Georgia in the early 1940s, children without a father were considered "less-than." Families without strong father figures were sometimes mistreated. Children from families with daddies made $4.00 a day to work in the fields. I made $2.50 a day. Unscrupulous hirers and other males in the community took further advantage by fondling me as I walked to the tobacco fields in the morning and as I walked home in the evening.

Between the ages of five and nine, I was abused regularly by male neighbors who were not members of our family. Even though family members commit 88 percent of abuse, that wasn't true in my case. My mother was not aware of what was happening. My brothers and sisters were not aware. Even my best friend, Elizabeth Jones, did not know, although years later, she reflected on my having been so sad, so often, that she knew "something" was wrong. Elizabeth remembers my trying to talk to her on several occasions and not being able to get the words out or to explain my problems. You see, children don't expect those in authority—those adults we have been ordered to trust, respect, and obey—to be capable of the horrors they often commit, especially when the abusers are churchgoing people. Nobody suspected their indiscretions.

I did not tell anyone anything about the abuse for more than thirty years. I, like others who have felt the shame and pain of looking back and seeing that we did nothing to stop it, was rendered mute. You see, I could not take up for myself because I did not know how—nor did I know how to ask anyone for help. Statistics often show that when abused children do tell, they are not believed or accepted. If I had told, I might have been put into a mental hospital as some children were. Research has revealed that many emotionally abused victims are labeled as mentally ill and placed in mental institutions. I discovered this from years of observing people in institutions and talking with leaders in the mental health profession.

I was intimidated by unbelievably cruel threats about what would happen to me if I told—or what would happen to members of my family if anyone found out. *It had to be our secret.* "Besides," I was told, "no one will believe you." I was convinced that "it" (this probing, pushing, panting, pawing, and peeking) was my fault and that everyone would know how really "bad" I was if I said *anything* to *anyone*. The people I loved the most were used to threaten me into silence. The men who were doing that to me were respected leaders in our community. Who would believe a child over them?

Hope and healing

This book is not about abuse. This book is about hope and healing and overcoming. No one can change her yesterdays, but everyone can form her future. The challenge is that many people have no hope, and without hope there is little chance for healing. Without hope there is no reason to move.

The majority of those who are hopeless have been abused— physically, sexually, spiritually, verbally, and, of course, emotionally. This book looks at the horror of abuse that leads to hopelessness and helplessness. But the main focus is on hope and healing, forgiving and living. This book will put a plan in place so that anyone will be able to come back from any adversity. "Coming back" is a decision only you can make.

Andrew Carnegie was responsible for developing more million-aires than anyone else. Someone once asked him, "What kind of people do you look for to become millionaires?" Mr. Carnegie stated, "Those who mine gold move tons of dirt to get to the gold." You and I will do the same. We need to continue digging until we get to the gold that we *know* is there. We need to deal with the obstacles that get in the way. We are looking for the gold—the gold of healing.

There are several types of abuse, and we are going to explore each of the major ones to raise awareness of the similarities of abuse. In the process, I am going to share my story with you as I know and remember it. In 1987 I began letting others know that I was abused as a child. Since that time, hundreds of women have come to me with their stories of tragedy, trauma, and shame.

No one wants to hear about abuse

For nearly twenty years, I have known this book had to be written. The more others said "Don't do it," the more I knew I had to. The naysayers may say I wrote this because I am stubborn, and they would be partially correct. But even more than that, the abused children, women, and men I have spoken with helped me realize that I could never reach as many people with my speeches alone. Through this book, I am reaching out to

- all of you who need someone to believe in and help you; I offer myself, Mamie Claire Darlington McCullough.

- all of you who don't know (or didn't know) how to ask for help.

- all of you who carry needless guilt, negative self-esteem, shame, pointless pain, and unnecessary limitations. Those terrible feelings are wasted energy and squandered resources in the battles you face daily.

Within these pages are the tools, the encouragement, and the opportunity to help change a life and help win the war. My hope is that those readers who have not suffered abuse will be equipped to encourage and help in the healing process of those who have suffered abuse. And my hope is that if you are an abuser, you will find yourself in these pages and seek the help necessary. You do not have to continue abusing another of God's own children.

Together: abused, abuser, male, female, old, young, friends, and loved ones, we can break this sickening cycle. Let's do it—together we can.

You make the decision to go

As much as I want you to go with me on this journey of hope and healing, I cannot talk you into doing so. *You* must make the decision to go. As my husband and I travel on my speaking circuit, we often go through poverty-stricken parts of the city, areas of the countryside, counties within states, or regions of the world. We go because we have a goal in mind. Our goal is not to travel through the unpleasant; rather it is to arrive safely at our destination, and then to continue the journey with hope, healing, and happiness.

In this book I provide a road map that will help lead you out of the maze of despair, depression, and despondency, but using the map is up to you. Don't travel this road simply because your spouse, parent, friend, or *any other person* in your life has encouraged you to do so. Travel with me *only* if you have made the decision to go. My commitment to you is one of privacy and belief in you, a person of respect, dignity and value.

I am very sorry to say that many women who read this book will find themselves somewhere in these pages. If there were ever a subject I would pray you couldn't relate to, it would be this one. Sadly, many of your stories are in this book; happily, however, together we can focus away from horror and toward hope and healing.

Fasten your seatbelt, because we are going on an emotional roller-coaster ride over these pages. The ride itself may not always be fun, but you will be glad when you reach the end. You will have a set of experiences and insights that you can use as you move forward in your life—whether you are in the process of healing or of helping others heal.

You are in the right place at the right time. You are a person of value and worth. If I had a $100 bill and asked you if you wanted it, you would most likely say yes. What if I crumpled it up? Would you still want it? Yes. What if I put it in the garbage can for a few days? Would you still want it? Of course you would, because the value would not have changed. It would still be worth $100. Your worth is far above $100; it is far above rubies, and you will always have value. No matter how crumpled up, wrinkled, soiled, or unjustly treated you've been, you can make the decision to get up, brush yourself off, and go forward. Always remember that you have value no matter, no matter, no matter. I believe in you.

I was much too far out all my life

Some friends—I'll call them Jack and Mary—were vacationing in the Caribbean, when Jack decided to go for a swim. Mary sat on the deck of the beach house to keep an eye on their children, who were playing nearby in the sand. From time to time, Jack would wave to Mary and she would wave back. She thought it was sweet of him to take the time to say "hello" to her and the kids. Jack had swum out too far and was frantically trying to signal his wife for help. He finally quit waving and struggled to make his way to the shore. As he fell exhausted onto the beach, Mary came running to see what was wrong.

"Why didn't you answer my plea for help?" Jack asked.

"I thought you were just waving to say hello."

Sometimes we feel that we are in water too deep and no one can help us. We feel overwhelmed, as if we're going under for the third time. There is no magic formula to make it all better, and each of us has to work through it one stroke at a time.

Many of our decisions put us away from the shore, but if we take action, we can make it to safety.

Chapter 2

Poor but Proud

I was born Mamie Claire Darlington on April 3, 1939, in rural South Georgia. Three years later, my father, a sharecropper, died, and we moved to the little town of Dixie, Georgia, which is between Thomasville and Valdosta on Highway 84. In Dixie, Mama bought a small, two-story home that had never had a coat of paint. She purchased it for $250 by paying ten dollars a month for it. I wasn't raised poor—I was raised p-o-r-e. The difference is that when you're poor, most of the people around you are just as destitute, but being p-o-r-e is when folks up on the hard road (the paved road) have a lot more than you do, and you know it. Also, all those "rich" folks up on the hard road have indoor plumbing and you're still walking the path to the outhouse. We Darlingtons never had it very easy in life, but who does? Mama always had a positive perspective and was committed to taking care of all nine of us children—six girls and three boys all under age seventeen. She had made the decision to keep us together and to be there for each one of us.

Even though I had a mother and brothers and sisters with strong character and courage who pulled us through rough times, I often

It's not where you start

felt I was living in a hopeless situation. I was convinced that I would never amount to anything because my mother had no education, because I had so many brothers and sisters, and because that was the way people saw me. But primarily I felt like a nobody because of verbal, sexual, and emotional abuse.

I used to dream of being rich one day. My idea of rich was having a house with a coat of paint on it and windows with screens. My house in Dallas, Texas, has paint and screened windows, so I guess I'm rich. I thank God every day for the little things in life. To me, it's the little things that make a difference. Little things make a good friend a great friend, a good parent a great parent, and a good relationship a great relationship.

When, where, or who you were born does not determine your success. Success is determined by what is on the inside. I often say, "I'm artificial on the outside, but real on the inside." (You *do* realize my hair is chemically dependent.) It isn't where we start that is important; it's where we end up. General Douglas MacArthur wisely said that security is an inside job. Too many of us waste a lifetime blaming our inadequacies and lack of determination on our parents or our circumstances. We play the blame game. We say, "If things had been different" or "If I were younger or older or taller" or "If my parents hadn't gone through a divorce," then everything would be better. We are all responsible for what we are and what we become. Being happy and successful is an attitude of belief and commitment.

I believe each of us is born with a hope-o-meter. No one knows what this mechanism looks like, but it's there inside each of us nonetheless. Some people have allowed their hope-o-meters to suffer from neglect and rust out. Regardless of the condition of your hope-o-meter, I believe you can get it working again.

You must s-t-a-r-t

Even though my mama could not read or write, she still taught us the basic lessons of life. I didn't realize this until I became a high-school principal and the newspaper came out with an article headlined "Old-fashioned principal teaches old-fashioned principles." The paper quoted me as saying that Mama taught us five basic things: (1) Work hard, (2) stay clean, (3) love others, (4) go to church, and (5) forgive others.

That's the culture in which I grew up. I never thought I would get out of Dixie, Georgia. I thought I would stay there for the rest of my life. I assumed that some man might ask me to marry him and we would have a bunch of kids and stay right there. But I had two things going for me. I loved the Lord and believed what the Bible said in Philippians 4:13, "I can do everything through him who gives me strength" (NIV), and I had the dream of a better life even though I did not know what it would lead to or where. That was all I needed to keep my hope-o-meter activated. Even though I did not hear about the bumblebee until I was thirty-four, I think I have lived this concept because of my deep faith.

I can fly

According to aerodynamics, the bumblebee shouldn't be able to fly because his wings are too light and his body is too heavy. He does not know this, however, so he flies anyway. I identify with the bumblebee, because I shouldn't be able to fly either, because of the challenges I've had throughout my life. But God has enabled me to fly successfully through a full, happy life. The symbol of the bumblebee is an important reminder to me that I make a daily decision to "bee" my best and go forward in faith. Belief brings me hope in doing what we often think we can't. I believe when we keep trying, regardless of circumstances, we become better—and *that* brings us hope.

Many of you feel that the hurt is too deep to heal and the journey too long. My desire is to give you both tools and permission to begin your journey of healing, to overcome your circumstances, and to fly through life. God wants you to *bee* all that you can *bee*—and so do I. Remember, I believe in you.

If you've read one of my books, *I Can—You Can Too* or *Get It Together*, you've heard much of my story. But since their publication, I have felt a need to add ideas to my story to help keep your head above water. I believe there's a good possibility that this book will help to give closure to your past and reactivate your hope-o-meter. We all need help at times. Perhaps this book can be your life jacket.

From the time I was born, my life has been a series of ups and downs. At age six, I started school with the hope of an education that would take me beyond that of my beginnings. The abuse had started before then, and it continued for the next several years, changing my life forever. When I reached fourth grade, I began to outfox my abusers. Even so, a feeling of inferiority—a feeling that I wasn't good enough—still followed me wherever I went. Guilt and shame were part of my everyday life.

In high school I played on the girls' basketball team, and we had a great team. I had no time for hobbies because I always held after-school jobs, but even though I was extremely shy, I began to date. The elated feeling I had from having a high-school sweetheart ended when, shortly after high school, we broke up. At that point, I wasn't sure exactly what it was I wanted out of life or how to get it. I only knew I wanted to be better. I worked for a while, and then traveled a thousand miles away from home to attend college. I heard there was a Christian college where I could work my way through school. After a thirty-six-hour bus ride, I arrived in Brownwood, Texas. The next day, I registered at Howard Payne University.

There were three important things I did not know about college: (1) I had to major, (2) I had to minor, and (3) I had to pay.

I'm Not Waving... I'm Drowning

Thinking I would drop out and return home, I went to the president of the college. But God had other ideas. Dr. Guy D. Newman and his wife, Estelle, helped me get started. They took me in for my freshman year and helped me get a good job. A local businessman hired me as a secretary, and I learned about business—my major—in the process. I listened, watched, and read. I attended charm school and earned extra money baby-sitting to buy nice clothes. I was surrounded by well-educated people. I was voted Most Pleasing to Behold (meaning best-dressed) by the student body. What a change from the poor little girl from Dixie, Georgia! I graduated from college with a business and teaching degree and immediately went to work full time for Herman Bennett of Brownwood, Texas, who managed apartments and built homes, hotels, and motels.

Soon after, in the fall of 1968, I met and married a man from Brownwood and continued working for Bennett Construction Company. My new husband wasn't happy, however, and after only five months the marriage ended in divorce. He told me he wanted no part of my life, my family, or my church. He did not love me. He wanted to leave and he did. I learned through this experience that it's impossible to make anyone love me. Rejection and verbal abuse contributed to my feelings of inferiority for a long time.

In 1970, I took a teaching job in my hometown of Dixie. Don McCullough, whom I had known previously, came back into my life and proposed to me. We were married on June 4, 1971, in the Dixie Baptist Church. I gave birth to our first child, Patti, in March 1973. Our second child, Brian, arrived in April 1975, and Jennifer, our third child, was born in September 1976.

After my first child was born, I returned to teaching high school and took a part-time sales job. I attended a seminar at which Zig Ziglar was the motivational speaker, and after writing the first I Can course (based on book *See You at the Top*), I moved with my husband to Dallas in 1979, to work for the Zig Ziglar Corporation in the education department. Shortly after we moved to Dallas, my husband died of a sudden heart attack at age forty-six. We had only been married ten years, and our children were eight, six, and five. I suddenly felt like I was drowning. I was a forty-two-year-old widow with three children to raise.

I've had a lot of years to observe and experience problems of all types and to learn how to respond to them. I believe the conclusions I've come to are valid:

- We will more than likely experience some rough spots or bumps in life, so we need to avoid as many potholes in the road as possible, prepare to absorb the shocks, and press on to our destination.

- It's not what happens *to* us that matters, but it's what we *make* of it. It is a decision we make.

- We can assuredly learn to live vicariously. We do not need to experience every problem to know that problems will hurt us.

I will admit that I made some wrong choices and had to suffer the consequences.

When I speak, I often sense—and am often told—that many in my audiences have gone through some of the same things I did. This book is for those people—maybe you or someone you know. My prayer is that what you read in the pages of this book will help you overcome and bring closure to the pain of the past and that you will find the hope, happiness, peace, and joy I've found.

Today is the best day of my life because I decided it would be. I believe we can be the best we can each day. If I have learned anything in the past few years, it is that my basic freedom is the freedom of choice. I can *choose* to make today the best day of my life, regardless of my circumstances. So can you.

We decide what kind of day we will experience and ultimately what kind of life we will lead. Along with each choice we make comes a consequence. Mary Crowley, a great Christian business-woman and the founder of Home Interiors and Gifts, once said, "We are free to the point of choice, then the choice controls the chooser."

Life is tough. I wish I could say the last few years for me have been perfect, but I can't say that. Life is not perfect. Dr. Scott Peck began his book *The Road Less Traveled* with the phrase "Life is difficult." Even though that statement may seem simple and obvious, it is nonetheless true. But before we all throw up our hands and invite everyone to our pity party, let me quickly add that there is good news. We can learn from every experience, whether good or not so good. If we maintain the proper perspective, each experience can be a learning opportunity. *Grow* through life—don't just *go* through life. Life is made of sunshine and rain, and both are required to make a rainbow. There are no mountains without valleys. My prayer is that you will find encouragement in the pages of this book. You will know that someone else has gone through similar pain yet lives to say, "This is the best day of my life. I'm going to live it to the fullest."

Yes, I've worked in the cotton fields, picked tobacco, and eaten beans for weeks. I've been depressed, abused, divorced, and widowed. I've even survived cancer. However, I'll never have to live those exact days again, just as you will never have to live those hard, hurtful days of your past again. Those experiences are over, and it's time to live the present to the fullest and reach toward the future with hope.

Chapter 3

The Ultimate Betrayal

From the first time I can remember, I wanted someone to take up for me. It's been difficult having had no father in my life since the age of three. But I did have a Father all along who watched over me as a baby and each day of my life—a heavenly Father. He is my Shepherd, Counselor, Comforter, and Future.

When I began writing my first book in 1988, it was written to help people "*bee* the best" they can be by encouraging them to use all their talents, abilities, and efforts. All my books have been written to give encouragement and to offer common-sense ideas to replace negative information from the past.

Even though abuse is a subject that most people will not or do not discuss, it is a subject that needs to be addressed, particularly in the family unit. My objective is the "so what." We all have seen in newspapers and on television much publicized stars and talk show subjects covering the abuses in our society. These are certainly not new subjects, but the media have addressed them, and we are more prone now to believe that these horrendous acts of crime *do* exist and that guilty parties should be confronted and punished.

I don't want to deal in the unpleasant details of every kind of abuse. Instead, I want to identify the different areas of abuse and help you overcome abuse's cruel effects. I want to help you feel like a person of worth and acceptance, one who is worthy of unconditional love. Replacing the garbage that others have placed on us is something I dealt with for many years, and I have only, in the writing of this book, been able to actually turn loose and identify some of the false ideas introduced into my life as a young child. These harmful and injurious ideas were placed in my life by people respected in the community. The word *respect* has new meaning for me as an adult. My goal is to replace the negative thoughts and feelings from the past with positive, healing words of encouragement and to help you keep on going, to help you make the most of what life has to offer.

I believe there are a lot of people in our society who are not necessarily *sick* wanting to get well; rather, they are *stuck* wanting to get on with their lives. Many people—married, single, young, old—feel trapped and frustrated with their lives and do not know how to get going or to get unstuck so that they can move on and upward.

Recently I was talking with a friend who is a therapist. She asked me to remember one time in my life that stood out in my memory. Immediately I envisioned a five-year-old child sitting on a dirt road in a small town. This five-year-old was crying. She was dirty, no shoes, a flour-sack dress, dirty hair. She was sitting, her arms around her knees, crying. This is the memory that stands out in my mind from my past. In actuality, this is probably when the abuse began. I don't know, but I do see myself as that lonely, hopeless-looking child with the feeling that she had no one to take up for her.

From my own experiences of abuse as a child, from the age of five to the age of nine, I was continually threatened and abused by some family friends. The mental pictures, the verbal threats, and the physical and emotional damage are all part of me, along with feelings of helplessness, hopelessness, defeat, and depression. (Some of you will definitely relate to many of my feelings.)

As one of nine children living in a small southern town, I felt like a nobody from nowhere because of the abuse I suffered at the hands of my perpetrators. The road has been rough and rocky many times and has had many side trips, some good and some not-so-good choices. I'll be the first to express to you that I'm never looking to play the blame game; nevertheless, I *have* been affected by the people in my life. My past is a part of me and will be a part of my future only to the extent that I allow others to continually control my future. That is true for you as well.

Families of today lead busy lives with the stresses of jobs, education, marital and social problems. Yet looking back to when we were young, we can readily see the stresses we coped with even as young children. No matter our age, we all need others with whom we can share our deepest thoughts, burdens, and celebrations of life.

Parents naturally want children to be safe, secure, and happy. However, there are many decisions we make in life that sometimes don't turn out as we think they should. Sometimes, too, our children's perceptions can be misleading to us as parents, teachers, and adults. We need to keep in mind that there are some precautions we need to take to keep our children safe physically, mentally, and spiritually. When a high-profile movie star or spiritual leader comes out with abuse in the tabloids, newspapers, and magazines, we all stand up and acknowledge what happened to them, and people are outraged. However, many of these same things are happening to our children in our own communities on a daily basis that we also need to acknowledge. For example, we need to take extra precautions in hiring caregivers or others who spend a great deal of time with our children. Sadly, however, much of the abuse comes from within the home, from close family and relatives.

I don't want you to become suspicious of everyone, but it is just common sense to ask the right questions, do some background checks, and be discerning about the people we trust with our children. I found out recently that even in many of our churches, nursery workers and teachers who work with children are required to

What can I do to protect my children from potential harm?

have background checks. This may seem intimidating, but this is a wise decision.

You may be wondering, *What can I do to protect my children from potential harm?* Here are some things you need to consider when you are raising your children, whether you are a stay-at-home mom, a working mom with children in day care, or a mom who has someone come in to take care of your children.

- Always ask, "Are there any objections to my doing a background check on you for any reason?" If the potential caregiver is innocent, she or he will agree to the check. I would encourage you to check references, especially with regard to any kind of sex offenses or other red flags. There is a sex offender registry, and a person's criminal history is not hard to find. There is a weekly sex offender list with names and addresses published in the Dallas newspaper. There are many, many ways that you can check. You can ask your local police or law enforcement agencies, no matter what size town you are in, how to do it. Personal references are recommended.

- It's also important for you to be specific in asking what the qualifications are. Be sure you interview past employers, going back ten years if possible.

- I would encourage you also to observe the way your potential caregiver or teacher relates to your children in whatever setting she or he will be working. I have found in raising my three that there are a lot of things the children can ask without the interviewee even knowing that you are checking things out. It's a good idea to ask your children after they talked with her how they feel about this potential caregiver. Children have a keen perception about people. I had to have a live-in housekeeper/childcare person for twelve years, and I wish I had known some facts beforehand.

- I would have the potential caregiver fill out an application with name, address, phone numbers, driver's license, references, and recommendations. Then check all the numbers, just to be sure.

- Also, ask her how she will get to work and who will bring her. (Sometimes that might cause a problem if she plans to have a relative or friend bring her—that would give a stranger access to your home or children.)

- Be aware of any red flags that could be potential problems before you make a final decision.

I believe in talking with your children regularly. When my children were growing up, we would sit around the dinner table at night. My rule was that nobody left until everyone was finished, and if I had something that I wanted to talk to my children about concerning safety or whatever, I would find a way to address that issue. My children are grown now, and they have said many times now that they knew what I was trying to do, but I found out what I needed to know. Many times, our talks were simply to make the children aware of precautions and to be careful.

As parents, teachers, colleagues, and neighbors, we want our children to be safe. I don't think that it is being suspicious, hard, or cruel. It is being factual in the day in which we live and is a way of staying connected. I do want to encourage you as parents to be thorough in checking on the people who will have input in your children's lives at home, church, school, and anywhere else.

It's important, too, to have a support system of some kind in place. The value of friendship is immeasurable. Close friends will hold us accountable and be there when we need them.

Something we need to understand is that we all need people, we all need friends, we all need fellow workers, and we all need a support system that can keep us accountable and help us to stay on the right track. Our needs are designed to drive us to growth. I like to say it this way:

We *grow* through life, not *go* through life. We need to be around people and friends who encourage us to grow. I always encourage people when they get in a down mood to pick up the phone and call somebody and talk to someone about their problems. This always seems to help me realize that my problems are not so bad after all. I also encourage you to be around people that are open to your asking for help.

One of the things that I discovered in my adult life is the value of asking other people to help me. I don't know why—I cannot explain it, but early on I evidently wanted to be independent and self-sufficient. I wanted to do everything myself so I would never look weak or, worse, inadequate. Some of this probably comes from the fact that I felt hopeless, trapped, ashamed, guilty, and not good enough as a child; I felt that I couldn't get out of the situation I was in. As a consequence of the deceit and improper actions of others toward me, I didn't know how to handle some of the problems that arose in my adult life. I wish I had all the answers, but I only have a few that might help you or someone you know.

One of those problems arose when I was in my late thirties and found out I was pregnant with my third child, Jennifer. Patti was three years old, and Brian was not yet one. Doctors suggested that I might consider terminating the pregnancy because it would be detrimental to my health, because the child may not be healthy, because of my age. They listed all the reasons why I should. However, because of my basic principles, I felt that I had no choice but to have the child. I was working at two jobs and trying to help juggle the world, so to speak, teaching a Sunday-school class and high-school business. I was busy, but I felt that abortion was not an option. My decision was right. My baby Jennifer grew up to be a special young woman, living for Jesus. She is in seminary and working as a preteen youth minister in our church.

In 1976, before Jennifer was born, I went to Atlanta to attend a business meeting I will never forget. I was on the twelfth floor of the Hilton Hotel, and I woke up petrified about 2:00 A.M. My heart palpitated. I felt hot and edgy. I had to get out of the hotel and out into the fresh air. The hotel windows would not open, so I had to dress and go downstairs. That was the beginning, and for the next five or six years, I suffered from extreme claustrophobia. A closed room, an elevator, a dark hall would cause anxieties to return. I felt like I was coming unglued. Claustrophobia is one of the manifestations of abuse as a child. Sometimes the feelings that we experienced as children come to the forefront again when we become adults. This was the case with my experience of claustrophobia. Even after I began speaking and traveling while I was working with Zig Ziglar, I could not stay in a hotel with secured windows. I would have to sit in the lobby or lie down on a couch in the lobby. I just could not handle a closed room. With much prayer, study, and help from special friends and counseling, I was eventually set free from this problem.

Friends came alongside and said to me, "You can make it. You can make it. I know you can." It took a lot of healing for that problem, but it's been under control now for twenty years. Even though I still experience twinges of occasional fright when I get exhausted and tired, I put my eyes on God, who is the great Healer. I continually look up to Him for help. Oh, the blessedness of friendship and the love of people who continue to surround me regardless of my frailties, inadequacies, and weaknesses.

I want to encourage you to develop wonderful friendships. My friend Elizabeth Jones has been one of my good friends since first grade, and that has been many, many years ago. How wonderful it is through the years that we have kept in touch. We can share, build each other up, and encourage one another in an honest, sincere, longtime relationship. I want to encourage you to surround yourself with those friends who will lift you up and be an encouragement to you. I believe that the most comforting people in the world are those who have been comforted, that the people who are the most understanding are the people who have been understood, and that the most loving people are those who have been loved.

God loves us all. It is up to us to remember who we are and to turn our lives over to Him on a daily—sometimes moment by moment—basis. We need to realize that He is a God of love and that He understands us, whether we understand our lives or not. What we receive, we want to give out. When we receive love, we want to give love. This is the reason I started the Encourager Foundation, to help friends like you and your loved ones through recovery. This is our mission statement:

> The mission and purpose of the Encourager Foundation is to carry a message of God's love, hope and caring to women in ministry, as well as abused women and hurting children.... It is our belief that through sharing a message of inspiration, either in person, through tapes, books and other resources, we can bring encouragement to a group of people who are in desperate need of believing in themselves once again.

The wonderful, most talented, intelligent women that serve on my board are Dr. Mary Allen, Mrs. Helen Applefield, Mrs. Helen Beasely, Dr. Millie Cooper, Ms. Guinell Freeman, Mrs. Jeanne Grubbs, Mrs. Barbara Hammond, Ms. Ann Hutchens, Ms. Elizabeth Jones, Mrs. Jennifer Krupa, Ms. Mavis Moore, Mrs. Jennifer McCullough, Dr. Hattie Myles, Mrs. Sharon Parker, J'nette Pattillo, Mrs. Francis Phillips, Dr. Grace Pilot, Mrs. Joyce Rowe, Mrs. Sondra Saunders, Mrs. Louise Sharp, Mrs. Cindy Skelton, Mrs. Sandi Smith, Mrs. Diane Tate, Dr. Velma Walker, and Mrs. Patti Wyman. These women are models of excellence for me. I value their friendship, encouragement, and love.

I heard a story recently about an artist who would look at the model and then draw, look at the model and then draw. Any of you who have ever taken even Sketching 101 in college, knows this is true.

I am a part of all that I have met.

Alfred Lord Tennyson

(I took art so I would not have to take speech.) I remember that we would stand for hours and look at the model of whatever we were drawing, whether it was a face, a leaf, or a person. I thought about what it would be like to draw a picture of the best example of love. We would have to look at Jesus Christ, and when we began drawing, we would look at the features, we'd draw a little bit; we'd look at the features, we'd draw a little bit more. I believe that when we want to know the perfect model as a friend or colleague that we should look at Jesus, and if we can't make a decision, we need to look back and see what He looks like or what He would have done or what He would have said. If we do that, we'd always be pretty much on target.

Several years ago, and it's still popular today, there was a phrase that the young people wore on bracelets or necklaces: W.W.J.D. It's a reminder that we should take the time to ask "What would Jesus do?" How would He handle it? Would He be loving? Would He be kind? How would He respond to this? I realize we cannot be just like Jesus, but that can be our goal. Life is a process. We never really reach the end of processing things in our lives.

Some people are in therapy for a very long time. A former Miss America, who tells of her incest as a child, stated that she went to more than fifty psychologists in her attempt to discover why she was the victim and how she could recover. What people don't understand, and as Tennyson once said, "I am a part of all that we have met." I believe we have to understand that the things that have happened to us are a part of us. My experiences are like a twenty-year-old scar that I have on my hand—I do not dwell on that scar, but if I focused on it and dwelt on it enough, I could actually relive the pain and see the cut in my mind's eye.

We do not want to focus on past pain. We want to focus on healed hearts, healed heads, and healed emotions. This is the good language that we can pass on. Sometimes people say, "Well, this happened to you as a child—when will you ever be well?" And they ask, "Aren't you done with this now? Didn't you go to therapy last year?

When will this be over?" They will add, "Don't you think it is worse since you have told it?" or "Don't you think it is worse since you started therapy?" And sometimes they say, "You need to have a deadline on when your emotions will heal." But we don't know that. They think when we are hurt so badly that we are like light bulbs that burn out. Replace them and there's light again. They think that the hurting and healing process can be fixed that easily, but certainly it is not that way.

In America, over 1 million children were abused this year. The abuse documented refers to physical abuse and neglect. However, I believe abuse can be extended beyond these two categories, which would cause the numbers to rise considerably. There are several different kinds of abuse, and the major ones I am aware of are covered in the next chapter.

I recently read an article in the paper about a research project on child abuse. In the study, the researchers are working with the theory that children could be responsible for their own abuse. That is insane.

The effect of child abuse lasts a lifetime. The physical, external abuse may heal, but the emotional trauma remains long after the physical. We often carry these feelings and fears throughout life, and many times the effects do not surface until later on, perhaps even when we become parents. Some abused children grow up to become abusive themselves.

Statistics show that

- over 75 percent of children who are victimized within the home have mothers who were victims.

- 75 percent of teenage prostitutes were molested as children

Some of the lifelong effects of child abuse are

- poor self-image

- disruptive behavior

- failure in school

- drug and alcohol abuse

- inability to depend on or trust others

- passive behavior

- obesity

- suicide

- blocked memories

- depression

While my child abuse lasted from age five to age nine, and even though it was fifty years ago, I can recall painful abuse by a particular smell of tobacco or house odors. The fact that I was told I was a "nobody" still rings in my ears, even today. That damaging word entered my soul as a child, and it remains there still. I never shared the devastating effect on me until I was older—when I read in the paper that child abuse was prevalent in small towns. Until then, I believed that I was alone in my abuse.

I found out, though, that abuse can and does happen in all types of homes—poor, middle-class, wealthy, rural, suburban, urban, involving one or both parents or a family friend, and all races.

A recent article in the *Dallas Morning News* said that 77 percent of child abuse is perpetrated by the parents, 10 percent by strangers, 11 percent by relatives or family friends, and 2 percent by childcare or foster-care providers.

Our first priority should be to do all we can to protect our children from ever becoming victims of child abuse. Consider the vulnerability of a child, and then consider these ironic truths:

- To become a licensed driver, you have to take a class, pass a written examination, and pass a driving test. To become a parent, all you have to do is have a child.

- A child who is molested by an adult has neither knowledge of her rights nor money with which to hire an attorney. The adult offender, however, often has financial strength to protect himself with legal counsel, should he ever be accused of child abuse. The child seems to be the loser.

- In many states, a parent who has been guilty of violent abuse may go on living in the same home with the children if he or she agrees to attend counseling sessions. Many children have been maimed or killed during this so-called family readjustment period.

- Many times a caseworker who has been assigned to work with a family after a case of reported abuse finds that she must be counselor to both the abused child and the abusive parent. This often confuses matters and creates lopsided loyalties and biased judgments. One person cannot be all things to all people.

These circumstances are all sad but true. More direct action is needed. Parents should know who the families are that their children associate with; they should serve as chaperones and coaches and helpers for all the activities their youngsters are involved in; they should teach their children how to report any personal abuse; and they should support church and school programs that help educate both youngsters and adults regarding the laws and protective measures related to child abuse. Child abuse prevention is a national program, and I recommend you get involved.

Child abuse is a crime. Child abuse is also a moral, social, and psychological offense. The incidents I endured as a small child made me feel unworthy of people's love, respect, and trust. They made me shy and self-conscious. They made me frequently examine myself in the mirror of my mind and turn away from that mirror filled with self-loathing and personal disrespect. No one, but no one, should be allowed to make any child feel like that.

It never occurred to me to tell anyone. I didn't think that Mama and my sisters would be able to stand up to the terrible men. My father was dead, and my oldest brother was working in another city. There was no one to take up for me. All sorts of wild imaginings went thorough my head about what happened to bad little girls if they were found out. Would I go to jail? Would my family disown me? Would I be sent to reform school or the county home? I should be ashamed. I lived in terror. When I went to sleep, I often had nightmares. During the day, I clung to my sisters in dreadful fear that if I were ever alone, that evil man would grab me again.

In my youthful innocence, I never dreamed that other men might want to take advantage of me. About a month after that first incident, however, a man my family had known for a long time accosted me. He invited me into his family home and, when we were alone, touched me and exposed himself to me. When I did not report the incident to anyone, this man continued to corner me alone. Since he had access to all the places I went, and since I was afraid to tell anyone what was going on, this man took advantage of me numerous times over a five-year period.

It wasn't until I was about nine that I became smart enough and vocal enough to ward him off, but the terror I carried with me was a daily reminder. And as bad as those two men were, there was even a third man who, on occasion, also abused me. Miraculously, none of these incidents resulted in my being raped. Still, they worked to destroy my self-respect and to shatter my self-esteem.

Life's misfit

And so poor, homely Mamie Claire, who already felt ugly on the *outside*, began to feel equally ugly on the *inside*. Now, you may be thinking that all kids go through a stage when they look gangly, lose their baby teeth, and stay dirty. What's the big deal, eh? Well, the big deal was that I never grew out of that stage inwardly. In my mind, I was ugly my entire childhood. What made it worse was that my sister Martha Ann was beautiful.

Nobody ever called me ugly or homely. They would just see my sister and me coming and say, "Oh, look, it is pretty little Martha Ann and Mamie Claire." I thought that was my identity in life—pretty Martha Ann's sister. Outside I could smile and feign contentment, but inside I had no confidence or satisfaction about who I was. It took me years and years to overcome this problem of negative self-image and even now, at $59.95 plus tax, this feeling of inadequacy and poor self-esteem raises its ugly head.

You can see why I am a fanatic regarding the necessity to protect our children and the need to teach them how to avoid circumstances in which they might encounter abuse. I stress this to parents, teachers, and civic leaders. It simply cannot be emphasized too much. I know. I am speaking from experience.

Child abuse is not something new—but the topic has gained more public attention of late. This attention has resulted in some positive changes in our ways of dealing with this dilemma. We now have twenty-four-hour police hot lines to handle reports of child abuse. State and federal laws now demand that nurses, doctors, and educators report all cases of suspected child abuse. Locally and nationally funded programs provide family shelters, caseworker assistance, and psychological counseling for victims of child abuse. When I formed the Encourager Foundation several years ago, my purpose was to help abused women and children. This book is my way of creating awareness and help for those people.

I laud all of the marvelous innovations for dealing with this terrible situation. Nevertheless, I caution all parents and teachers not to be lulled into a state of complacency by thinking that it is somebody else's problem.

Society eventually pays the price for its passivity. Too many victims of child abuse grow a little bit older to haunt us with juvenile crime, drug and alcohol abuse, juvenile prostitution, and suicide.

The situation can't get better until we take a hard look at what's going on. Child abuse cuts across all social, economic, cultural, and ethnic lines. Investigative and protective efforts confined to the low end of the socioeconomic spectrum are doomed to failure.

As I stated before, child abuse is a crime. It may be a social problem; it may be the product of a disordered mind; it may indicate an overall family dysfunction—but it is always a crime. The public, however, generally does not view it that way. If someone viciously attacks a child on the street, the public wants the perpetrator prosecuted for assault. But if that same person commits the exact same act upon his own child in his own home, we call it child abuse and summon the social workers. A child killed by his parents is just as dead as a child killed by a stranger.

We must stop tolerating these crimes. There are changes that could be implemented immediately that would cost very little. Yet such changes would have a cosmic effect, not only on children currently being abused, but also upon the course of the nation for years to come. All that is required is that we look at the problem clearly and approach the issues with a unified sense of purpose. These nine guidelines could be implemented tomorrow:

1. All reported cases of child abuse should be investigated by professionally trained fact finders.

2. The current system of using the same social workers to simultaneously protect the child and rehabilitate the parent must be replaced by a mandate for separate teams.

3. We must protect children who are in danger and be strong enough to tell and help.

4. Children have a short life as children. We can no longer permit the endless cycle of removal, so-called rehabilitation, return to the family, continued abuse, removal, more rehabilitation, and so on. We must be proactive.

5. We should impose parenting standards on previous abusers and monitor the abusers to make sure they adhere to them.

6. The confidentiality of the family court must not be a shield to protect the abuser.

7. The government must be as accountable for child abuse as is the individual parent.

8. Each family adjudicated as abusive must be given every chance to reform, but not given an endless period of time.

9. Social workers must be psychiatrically screened before being allowed to work in the system.

Words of a pediatrician about verbal child abuse

"Your child trusts you and believes in you—so never tell your child he is bad or clumsy or stupid or anything else that will make him feel inferior."

Today
by Henry Matthew Ward

When I got mad and hit my child
"For his own good," I reconciled,
And then I realized my plight:
Today, I taught my child to fight.
When interrupted by the phone,
I said, "Tell them I'm not at home."
And then I thought, and had to sigh…
Today, I taught my child to lie.

The Ultimate Betrayal

I told the taxman what I made,
Forgetting cash was paid;
And then I blushed at this sad feat…
Today, I taught my child to cheat.
I smugly copied a cassette,
To keep me free of one more debt.
But now the bells of shame must peal…
Today, I taught my child to steal.
Today, I cursed another race.
Oh, God, protect what I debase,
For now, I fear it is too late.
Today, I taught my child to hate.
By my example, children learn
That I must lead in life's sojourn
In such a way that they be led
By what is done, not what is said
Today, I gave my child his due
By praises for him instead of rue.
And now I have begun my guide:
Today, I gave my child his pride.
I now have reconciled and paid to IRS on all I made.
And now I know that this dear youth
Today has learned from me, of truth.
The alms I give are not for show,
And yet, this child must surely know
That charity is worth the price;
Today, he saw my sacrifice.
I clasp within a warm embrace
My neighbor of another race—
The great commandment from above.
Today, I taught my child to love.
Someday, my child must face alone
This world of fearsome undertone,
But I have blazed a sure pathway:
Today, I taught my child…to pray.

Chapter 4

No Place to Hide

Due to the fact that some people do not realize that abuse exists or recognize it, I am going to list some of the types most prevalent in our society today. Perhaps these will help us to recognize the signs earlier on in our relationships with family and friends. I'm sure I have not addressed every type of abuse, but this is an attempt to create an overall awareness. The different abuses—as I understand them and as I have learned from the testimonies that have been shared with me—entail several kinds: physical, emotional, neglect, child, domestic, spiritual, verbal, sexual, alcohol and drug, and divorce.

Physical abuse: Brutal force

One night when I was four or five, my father stripped me naked and left me in the backyard. It was dark, and I was too small to know how to get out. I could only shiver and watch the bugs crawl over me. I don't know how long I was there. Finally, he came back and removed me.

My father wanted to have me completely under his control. He locked me in a rabbit cage, and another time tied my wrists and ankles to a cross. I remember him punching the right side of my face so hard it nearly shattered my jawbone.

Because my father used to choke me whenever I started to cry, as an adult I couldn't cry without choking. It took me four years to learn to shed tears. But my spirit was never taken away from me. I'd just hidden it someplace deep inside.

—Lori

We can often identify physical abuse more quickly than other kinds of abuse. The scratches, bruises, bumps, and broken bones can be seen and are harder to hide from teachers and friends. Injuries can lead to painful and serious medical problems. In some cases, the damage can lead to permanent disability, mental retardation, or even death. There are many types and levels of physical abuse, but my concern is that we be attentive to these atrocities and then take action to stop them.

Types of physical abuse include:

- pushing or shoving

- holding to keep from leaving

- slapping or biting

- kicking or choking

- hitting or punching

- throwing objects

- locking out of the house

- abandoning in dangerous places

- refusing to help when sick, injured, or pregnant

- subjecting to reckless driving

- forcing off the road or keeping from driving

- raping

- threatening or hurting with a weapon

- hitting with an object

- twisting or breaking an arm or leg

- banging head against the wall or floor

- tying down or locking in a room to keep from leaving

- confining to a closet or small area

My boyfriend abused me physically, verbally, sexually, and emotionally. He would hit me, choke me, pull my hair, and slap me when I wouldn't give in to his sexual demands. I was too naive to know what was happening, and I truly believed that this boy was the best I could get and that I was powerless, because that's what he told me. This happened years ago, and my parents still don't know about it.

—*Karen*

Emotional abuse: Is hurting better than nothing?

Attorney and author Andrew Vachss has devoted his life to protecting children. When asked to name the worst case of child abuse he ever handled, he said, "I think about it every day. My answer is that of all the forms of child abuse, emotional abuse may be the cruelest and longest-lasting of all." Vachss went on to say, in a 1994 article in *Parade* magazine:

Emotional abuse, the systematic diminishment of another, can be verbal or behavioral, active or passive, frequent or occasional. Regardless, it is often as painful as physical assault, and the pain often lasts longer. It may be intentional or subconscious (or both), but it is always a course of conduct, not a single event. It is designed to reduce a child's self-concept to the point where the victim considers himself unworthy of respect, friendship, love and protection. It can be as deliberate as a gunshot: 'You're fat. You're stupid. You're ugly.' Emotional abuse scars the heart and damages the soul. Like cancer, it does its most deadly work internally. Its victims' lives often are marked by a deep, pervasive sadness, a severely damaged self-concept and an inability to truly engage and bond with others.

Emotional abuse is the hardest area to identify because it cannot be seen and often is repressed for many years before it is dealt with. Children are dependent on adults for security, acceptance, love, and guidance. When adults harm them, their world becomes uncertain, frightening, and confusing. Emotional damage from abuse can stunt a child's emotional growth. Later in life, the child may not be able to show his or her feelings or understand others' feelings. His or her self-worth and capabilities are questioned.

> *My mom was not an encourager and often called us stupid, blaming us for the things she did not have. She told us she hated us and that we would never amount to anything. I have an eating disorder, have suffered from poor self-esteem, and have always believed that I could not accomplish anything. My siblings are alcoholics, living in abusive relationships, or have psychological problems. I have learned to look to God for significance, worth, and the strength to do His will.*
>
> *—Donna*

Types of emotional abuse include:

- ignoring feelings

- ridiculing or insulting

- withholding approval, appreciation, or affection as punishment

- continually criticizing, name-calling, shouting

- insulting or driving away friends or family

- humiliating in private or public

- refusing to socialize with

- keeping from working, controlling money, making all decisions

- refusing to work or share money

- taking car keys or money away

- regularly threatening to leave or telling to leave

- threatening physical harm

- punishing or depriving

- abusing pets

- threatening spouse with kidnap of the children in the event of escape

- manipulating with lies and contradictions

I have a long history of a controlling father who later murdered my mother and committed suicide. I have suffered from depression as a result. The laughter is gone. The innocence is gone.

*It is a long, hard road back to a healthy recovery, and I don't know
if full recovery is possible—but better is always possible.*
—Carol

Neglect: Orphans at home

We are often reminded in the newspaper or on television of the
terrible abuses inflicted on children, abuses such as molestation,
incest, and rape. These are horrible acts, but there is another abuse
that often goes unnoticed, unreported, and avoided—neglect, a lack
of love, care, and respect.

This abuse is often overlooked not only in the down-and-out
neighborhoods, but also in the best neighborhoods, the ones I call
the up-and-out. A child can live in a higher income household with
both parents and still be neglected. So let us be careful in pointing
our fingers at single, poor parents. It is certainly not only the lower-
income families that suffer from this kind of abuse.

Neglect means to fail to perform a duty, to fail to care for, to fail
to attend through carelessness or abandonment. Neglected children
often are thought of as without clothes, food, and other life essen-
tials, and I realize there are many of these in the world. These basics
are of course vitally important to life. There are other neglects, however, such as

- no expression of love, affection or respect

- no verbal praise or encouragement

- no communication

- no rules or boundaries; in other words, passive living

- being ignored by family members

- no validation of worth

When I was rearing my children, I realized that one of the right things I did in raising them was to have rules to live by. It gave them boundaries without taking their freedom away. I believe it gave them freedom to operate and make good choices.

A story of neglect

When I was two or three years old, my five-year-old brother woke me in the middle of the night to tell me Mommy and Daddy were gone. I crawled out of bed and tiptoed through our house in terror. We were the only ones there. We went back to our bedroom and huddled together on the floor, crying all night. When our parents came home from their night of drinking, they were angry that we weren't in bed.

—Judi

All of us—children and adults, young and old—need to be validated, affirmed, and loved. If we are neglected as children, we often spend our entire life looking for love and acceptance in all the wrong places and from the wrong kind of friends and mates.

Most of the problems that stem from hurts we have had in our lives are relational problems—getting along with people or having friends. You may know people that go from one problem to another or are influenced by the wrong kind of people. They get into destructive patterns of behavior. Many times I have discovered that these people have been hurt so deeply as children or as adults that they think they are not deserving of a good life. They get into relationships with people who hurt them even more. Grown children of alcoholics often marry alcoholics themselves. I believe these relational sins, as they are called, can be broken, but it takes a lot of work and effort on the part of the hurting person to stand back and see the destructive pattern they're in.

Domestic abuse: Looking for love at home

My husband was an alcoholic and would beat me up. I felt very trapped. At the time, there were no shelters. I'd make excuses for all the bruises and black eyes. Being abused makes you feel so worthless. It's hard to trust people after that. I've been single for a while now. I don't think I'll ever be the same.

—Betty

My dad is the most critical person I've ever seen. It is so-o-o heavy to be around him. I saw him wound, kill, my mom's spirit. It is beyond belief how a man can be so mean. It has killed her spirit beyond hope. I've watched him kill her desire to be generous. All she does is sit and watch television. She used to give, laugh, and share—and now she sits. It breaks my heart. I also suffer verbally, yet I know who I am in Christ, and I don't have to live with him anymore.

—Kathleen

Domestic abuse is a habit. It's familiar. It becomes normal to those who grow up witnessing their parents fighting—and often the father physically abusing the mother. Often the children are told they are bad or rotten and deserve it... and they believe it. The parent being abused is often cut off, afraid, and alone, with nowhere to go. To anyone reading this book, if you are in an abusive home situation, I suggest you remove yourself immediately. It doesn't get better—it only gets worse. I am not advocating divorce, because I believe that God hates divorce, but I am asking you to find a way to escape the abuse. There are safe places you can go. Your boundaries are important to help you to heal and keep your family safe from the horrendous acts of abuse. God grieves when you or your family members are abused, and I believe He will make a way for you to escape.

Marguerite was a victim of domestic abuse for years until she escaped her abusive live-in boyfriend with the help of a shelter for battered women. Now she volunteers at a local shelter for battered women and is working to establish a safe harbor for battered women in her area. Marguerite knows what it's like to need help getting out of abusive situations. She wants to make the break as easy as possible for other women like her. She says that shelters help women feel a part of something so they don't feel alone in their fight to get out of an abusive relationship. Many can't or won't go back to their families because the abuser shows up and threatens them with violence.

A shelter removes them from the threats because the location is kept secret. In this safe environment, a woman can begin the healing process. Many women return to the abuser because they feel they can't make it without him. There's an addictive attachment there that has to be broken—a dependency on the abuser that only time away and hope for change can break. That is why women's shelters and counseling programs are so important.

There are a number of ways you can protect yourself from an abusive husband or boyfriend:

- Prepare a survival kit. Include in it (1) clothes for yourself and the children for a two-week period, (2) cash to live on, (3) copies of the children's immunization and school records, (4) cosmetics and toiletries, and (5) toys and books for the children.

- Find someone to keep your survival kit, or place it in a storage locker across town until you need it. Never choose a close family member's home, the home of a mutual friend, or a neighbor's home. This makes them a target.

- Find out where you may go for help.

- Try to defuse his anger. Don't antagonize your mate by arguing or fighting back.

- Never pick up a weapon. He could use it on you since he's probably much stronger and could take it away.

- Don't run where the children are. He could harm them as well.

- Make yourself a smaller target. If you cannot avoid being hit, dive into the nearest corner and tuck yourself into the smallest ball you can. Draw up your legs to protect your body and cover your face with your arms around each side of your head, fingers entwined.

- Make your escape. If you've had a chance to call 911, have the police restrain the abuser while you take the children and leave. If you've been unable to call the police, slip out when he is asleep.

- Create a false trail. After escaping to a safe place and retrieving your survival kit, you can throw the abuser off your track until the courts or police deal with him.

- Call motels, schools, employment agencies and real estate rental agents in a town at least a six-hour drive away. Ask questions that will require calls back to your old home phone number. This will keep the abuser on a wild-goose chase while you get help from police, friends, and shelters.

The President's Crime Commission reports that domestic violence is America's number one underreported crime. Every fifteen seconds a woman is beaten. Battering is serious. Women may be verbally abused, slapped, kicked, punched, thrown, knifed, shot, or killed. The Centers for Disease Control and Prevention recently reported that attacks by husbands on wives result in more injuries requiring medical treatment than rapes, muggings, and auto accidents *combined*.

Twenty percent of all women visiting emergency rooms arrive there following a beating at home. FBI reports show that in over 50 percent of all battered women cases, the children are beaten as well. Twenty-five percent of all reported victims of domestic violence are pregnant women.

Women who stay trapped in an abusive relationship are too afraid to leave, they may be ashamed, or they may have no resources—or all of these may apply. These women need our help. Domestic violence happens in all communities. It happens as often in upper-class families as it does in lower-class families; it happens in families of all races and educational backgrounds.

In Dallas, a victim of family violence may seek a Protective Order from the Dallas County District Attorney's office when she decides to take that critically important step. This order prohibits a person who commits family violence from being within a certain distance of the victim and prohibits any further contact or abuse.

When a victim of family violence makes a decision to obtain help, a system needs to be in place to provide the victim with timely and responsive assistance. The Dallas County Commissioner's Court recently approved the Protective Order Rapid Response Team concept. This team is composed of major county departments that deal with the process of a Protective Order and has relocated certain departments in order to provide services at one central location.

Another major area of concern has been the time frame between filing the affidavit and serving the Notice of Protective Order on the respondent (the person alleged to have committed family violence). It is anticipated that this will improve from what was an average of twenty days to approximately two days.

When a victim makes the choice to take control of her or his particular situation and pursue protection, time is critical. By obtaining quicker service on the Respondent, this puts the Respondent on notice that violence will not be tolerated and that a court proceeding is scheduled and that certain penalties apply if the terms of the Order of the Court are violated. Now, because of the location and cooperation of different departments within the county, response time is shortened, which allows for quicker protection for the victim.

With this collaborative effort and a centralized location, the ease and efficiency with which victims can secure a Protective Order is greatly improved. The greatest need of family violence victims is their safety. Protective Orders are life saving.

Cycle of violence by a spouse or boyfriend

The cycle-of-violence theory makes it easy to understand how women become victimized, how they learned helplessness behavior, and why they do not attempt to escape. According to this theory, there are three phases (different in intensity and time for different couples).

1. Tension building:

   - During this phase, she attempts to calm the batterer.

   - She becomes nurturing and does not show anger because she believes that her action will prevent his anger from exploding.

   - She denies her own anger and rationalizes that perhaps she did deserve the abuse.

   - She has some control over the situation by controlling external circumstances (such as manipulating family members).

2. Acute battering incident:

   - This is characterized by letting all go—may have been battering in tension, but during this phase both accept that his rage is out of control.

   - This is usually briefer than two to twenty-four hours, although some women report a steady reign of terror.

- There is nothing she can do to prevent it. If she answers his verbal abuse, it angers him. If she remains quiet, it angers him.

- She remains isolated.

- Both prefer to get this stage over with because of what follows.

3. Honeymoon phase:

   - This phase is welcomed—the batterer exhibits extreme loving and kind behavior.

   - He begs forgiveness, and she wants to believe.

   - This is where the victimization becomes complete—she stays.

   - She is made to feel guilty.

   - She gets all the rewards of marriage.

15 warning signs of an abusive personality

If your mate or boyfriend is displaying any combination of the following behaviors, there's a good chance he is a potential batterer:

1. *Push for quick involvement.* He comes on very strong, claiming "I've never felt loved like this by anyone." An abuser pressures the woman for an exclusive commitment almost immediately.

2. *Jealousy.* The abuser is excessively possessive; calls constantly or visits unexpectedly; prevents you from going to work because "you might meet someone," checks mileage on your car.

3. *Controlling.* He interrogates you intensely (especially if you're late) about whom you talked to and where you were; keeps all the money; insists you ask permission to go anywhere or do anything.

4. *Unrealistic expectations.* He expects you to be the perfect woman and meet his every need.

5. *Isolation.* He tries to cut you off from family and friends; accuses people who are your supporters of "causing trouble." The abuser may deprive you of a phone or car or try to prevent you from holding a job.

6. *Blames others for problems and mistakes.* The boss, you—it's always someone else's fault if anything goes wrong.

7. *Makes everyone else responsible for his feelings.* The abuser says, "You make me angry" instead of "I am angry" or "You're hurting me by not doing what I tell you." Less obvious is "You make me happy."

8. *Hypersensitivity.* He is easily insulted, claiming that his feelings are hurt when he is really mad. He'll rant and rave about the injustices of things that are just part of life.

9. *Cruelty to animals and children.* He kills or punishes animals brutally. Also may expect children to do things that are far beyond their ability (whips a three-year-old child for wetting a diaper) or may tease them until they cry. Sixty-five percent of abusers who beat their partners will also abuse the children.

10. *"Playful" use of force during sex.* The abuser enjoys throwing you down or holding you down against your will during sex; says he finds the idea of rape exciting.

11. *Verbal abuse.* He constantly criticizes you or says blatantly cruel, hurtful things; he degrades you, curses you, and calls

you ugly names. This may also involve sleep deprivation, waking you up with relentless verbal abuse.

12. *Rigid sex roles.* He expects you to serve, obey and remain at home.

13. *Sudden mood swings.* He switches from sweetly loving to explosively violent in a matter of minutes.

14. *Past battering.* He admits hitting women in the past, but says they made him do it or the situation brought it on.

15. *Threats of violence.* The abuser makes statements like "I'll break your neck" or "I'll kill you" and then dismisses them with "Everybody talks that way" or "I didn't really mean it." If he has come this far, it is time to get help, or get out.

Spiritual abuse: As the steeple turns

All of us, as Christians, need to be on guard. Leaders are to protect and nurture the people. Paul urged the leaders of the early church to "keep watch over yourselves and all the flock" (Acts 20:28 NIV).

There are thousands of churches in the United States, of every denomination and creed. I believe being a member of a church or faith is very important; however, every religion perhaps is not what it seems or what we think it is.

Several years ago we all were made aware of a cult near Waco, Texas, where members were killed because of many wrong choices made by their leader. There have been many cults throughout the history of our country, but it does not mean that all churches are like this. In fact, these are certainly in the minority, not the majority.

Spiritual abuse may be the result of a misinterpretation of the Bible. The book of James states that spiritual leaders and teachers will be more harshly judged. I believe the reason for this is the importance of the leader's example, since followers tend to accept leaders as authoritative and above reproach.

I remember a situation with a local church in which the pastor was asked to leave because of infidelity. How sad that a talented minister had to be asked to leave because of this kind of choice. I believe that this kind of indiscretion is an abuse. The church members believed that what was being said on Sunday morning was being lived the rest of the week. When leaders give the impression of trying to be loyal, trustworthy, and godly—and deliberately do the opposite because of human choices—then it is abuse and is wrong. We have all heard the adage "no man is an island." When a spiritual leader falls, it affects everyone, especially the church body. Because of this, many people doubt the church and leave or move their membership. Families break up, and children become confused and puzzled about whom to believe. Our actions speak so loudly that others cannot hear what we are saying. Children are like sponges, and they grow up believing what we as adults tell them. They question their trust in the leadership and in God, and some perhaps may never return to the church.

What is spiritual abuse? *Spiritual abuse* is the mistreatment of a person who is in need of help, support or greater spiritual empowerment, with the result of weakening or decreasing that person's spiritual empowerment or faith.

Spiritual systems that teach or insinuate that even though you are saved, you are still worthless before God—"just a sinner saved by grace, a worm and not a person"—are spiritually abusive to their followers.

Learn to lean on Jesus and not on people. Proverbs 3:5 says, "Trust in the LORD with all your heart and lean not on your own understanding." Let the Word of God be your foundation. Know the Word and use it in your daily life as a guide.

In a Dear Abby column in the *Dallas Morning News*, Free At Last wrote in saying that she and her family belonged to a church for several years. She had wondered why they were asked to sacrifice so much more than other Christians from other churches. They were told that they were a special church with a special calling. They were ordered to give up any activity or relationship that would keep them from their church obligations or that planted seeds of doubts in their minds.

When things got a little too weird, she and her husband informed the pastor that they had decided to leave the church. He said that if they left, they would be doomed to divorce and that their kids would not serve God when they grew up. They lost all their friends—some they had known for over ten years. They later joined a church that does not try to control their lives, but the spiritual abuse of their former church took its toll on their lives.

If something feels uncomfortable spiritually in your place of worship or Bible group, it's time to examine it more closely and do something about it. No individual or organization should be controlling your life. Watch out for elitism—the idea that that particular group is "better than" or "more special than" other churches, organizations, or people. This superior attitude will not guide people. It will push them away. Remember, too, that the church's goal is to lead the people to the cross—not to nail them to it.

The Roman Catholic Church has come under much criticism because of allegations that several priests sexually abused altar boys in past years. Many times, allegedly, the abuse was covered up and the priests sent to other parishes, where the abuse continued.

Many of us are wondering, *Who can we trust?* When a Christian leader falls—especially one we greatly admire, one who may have had a great impact on our Christian walk—we feel betrayed and angry. We take it personally. The Body of Christ has been injured through the fall of some of the leaders, and we all feel the pain.

But we have to move beyond our feelings and look for lessons to be learned:

- We need to be sure not to judge others, assuming that we would never fall.

- We can help our brothers and sisters in Christ by praying for them as Paul exhorts us to do in Ephesians 6:18, "With this in mind, be alert and always keep praying for all the saints."

- We need to continue to trust in God and to not give up on our walk with Him because we've been hurt by someone else.

- We need to be consistent in attendance and tithes even though we may not feel like it. Being consistent and obedient always carries rewards.

The story of Dr. Jimmy Allen (former president of the Southern Baptist Convention) and his family's fight against AIDS is touching. They received little help or encouragement from the church—in fact they were ostracized from the church because of their son's condition. The AIDS virus entered their lives through a tainted transfusion that Dr. Allen's daughter-in-law received at the birth of her first son. Many times we judge with our worldly eyes, and we do not have that right. As fellow believers, we should love more and see others as God would see them—through spiritual eyes of concern, help, and caring.

> At the end of our lives, we will not be judged by how many diplomas we have received, how much money we have made or how many great things we have done. We will be judged by "I was hungry and you gave me to eat. I was naked and you clothed me. I was homeless and you took me in."... This is Christ in distressing disguise.
> —Mother Teresa

Verbal abuse: Sticks and stones may break my bones, but words break my heart

My husband, who was a minister, would make jokes about my appearance, habits, housekeeping, and mothering. He always had a putdown for the kids, made fun of them, berated them for their grades, and compared them to their friends. I had zero self-esteem. My daughter, even today, thinks she is dumb and has never felt she was good enough. My son has had stomach problems all his life from the stress of trying to please his father and never being good enough.

—Anna

Verbal abuse is the use of words to attack, injure, or degrade someone. The abuser's desire is to have power over another person. Men who beat their wives do so only about three to four times a year, but interspersed between those episodes is continual emotional and verbal abuse. The verbal abuse is the weapon used to control and to create a controlling environment so that the physical abuse can begin or continue.

I was told I was a nothing. I was told I'd be pregnant and married before I graduated from high school, despite the fact I didn't sleep around. I was told I was ugly, stupid, and because I came from a single parent, I was going to become one, too. I now have low self-esteem, and my theology is messed up.

—Vanessa

Having grown up believing that I was a nobody, it was strange to me when I heard positive words about myself for the first time. Back when I was attending college at Howard Payne University, I was riding in the backseat of Dr. and Mrs. Newman's car when I heard Dr. Newman say to his wife, "See—I told you she was bright!" Hearing those words changed something in me, and I began to believe in myself.

Children are all too often victims of verbal abuse, whether they suffer from putdowns, yelling, criticism or name-calling. In Laura's case, she doesn't remember the names she was called. She just has a strong memory of being yelled at and put down—a memory of being punished for being different. Today she feels dumb, ugly, and unloved, and she is anything but that. She's a beautiful, intelligent woman who is just now coming out of the pain of years of verbal abuse by her parents.

Every day, my stepmother told me I was fat, ugly, ditsy, and stupid. She said nothing would ever come of me. I moved out [to live with my mom] when I was 16 because I realized love and acceptance were more important than security. (My mom had not had a stable home or job.) I became a leader in my school, got good grades, and am now attending college. When I got saved at age 16, God helped me overcome. I was determined I was going to be somebody—somebody for God.

—Holly

Sexual abuse: Can I ever forget?

My stepfather raped me from the age of 8 to the age of 10—several times a week. I never got to be a child. Also, my innocence was taken away from me. My childhood trauma surfaced when I had my children.

—Lisa

A national survey of more than 1,200 adults found that 27 percent of the females and 16 percent of the males had been sexually victimized during childhood. Sexual abuse can occur from infancy through adolescence and appears to take place among all economic, religious, and ethnic groups.

I am a victim of incest. I don't remember much of anything before age twelve. It has just been in the past year and a half that I remember anything about it. I am thirty-one years old. I was told by my pastor to turn it over to God, but I'm not sure how to

do that. And if I'm giving all this to God, why am I so tormented inside? If He can't hear me and answer me, who can?
—Anonymous victim

If I could sit down and talk to this young woman, I would tell her that healing is not as simple as simply turning it over to God, but that's where we have to start. He is the One to guide us on this journey of hope and healing, and we have to be willing to go with Him. Sexual abuse can include:

- Telling anti-women jokes or making demeaning remarks.

- Treating women (or men) as sex objects.

- Being jealously angry, assuming you would have sex with any available man.

- Insisting you dress in a more sexual way than you want.

- Minimizing the importance of your feelings about sex.

- Criticizing you sexually.

- Insisting on unwanted and uncomfortable touching.

- Withholding sex and/or affection.

- Calling you sexual names like *whore* and *frigid*.

- Publicly showing sexual interest in other women.

- Having affairs with other women after agreeing to a monogamous relationship.

- Forcing sex with him or others or forcing you to watch others.

- Forcing particular unwanted sexual acts.

- Forcing sex after beating.

- Forcing sex when you are sick or your health is in danger.

- Forcing sex for the purpose of hurting you with objects or weapons.

- Committing sadistic sexual acts.

A family "friend" began sexually molesting me when I was 12 and continued until I was 15. My mother sexually approached me at age 14. This has caused the whole gamut of problems. It bothers me more to admit it has not only affected me, but everyone that I have ever had a relationship with.

—Iris

There are so many family secrets. No one would ever even have a clue what's happened. You always have this sense of loss— like something's been misplaced and you can never reclaim it— the precious gift of innocence. I've suffered from depression and thoughts of and attempted suicide. God has helped me. He saved me. I couldn't have survived without Him. I like to think I'm a work in progress. One day I'll be complete in heaven.

—Maria

Alcohol and drug abuse: Escape from reality

Alcoholism can challenge a family to the max.
—Renee

Whatever kinds of mind-altering drugs or alcohol an individual might use, these cripple his judgment and decisions—not to mention the tremendous financial strain it places on the person and his family. It often leads to legal problems and improper conduct such as stealing. Drug and alcohol abuse are physical, financial, and spiritual problems, and are considered by many to be sickness, mental disease, or habit.

My father was an alcoholic and never had much to do with me. When he was drunk, he became abusive—nagging, complaining, and physically abusive.

—Sharon

One in ten pregnant women uses drugs, leading to almost half a million babies born every year who are damaged by drugs and alcohol. Even kids who start out fine are at risk for drug use as adolescents, and counselors say they see kids as young as ten. Counselors agree that the most important thing a parent can do is to get educated about what drugs are out there, how they're used, and how they affect kids. If you have a problem or you suspect your child may have a problem, get help right away. Seek a counselor. Talk with school officials to seek help. My best advice is get help immediately. The bad habits do not just fade away; they escalate into worse habits and detrimental lifestyles.

My husband was a violent alcoholic. Seven months into my first pregnancy, he began drinking and abusing me. Fortunately, he did not drink all the time. He was a "binge" drinker. He usually got drunk on holidays. I was constantly covering up his drinking and abuse with people at work and church—even our family and friends. I was under unbelievable pressure and living in great fear. Sometimes he would be so violent, I would have to run for my life. At one point, I called the police when I knew he was coming home drunk to beat me up. (He had told me on the phone.) They said they could do nothing until he showed up there and beat me! It was a life of fear, but God sustained me. My husband seriously abused one of our children while I was gone, and I was told by the

Department of Health and Human Resources that I had to leave him if I wanted to keep my children. Now that we have been divorced for several years, I have seen my children grow up strong, happy, and serving the Lord. I am so thankful to Him for taking a dire situation and turning it into a blessing.

—Anonymous

Divorce: Goodbye love—hello Pop-Tarts

I was divorced several years ago after 18 years of marriage. My husband left after making the decision that he wanted a divorce. I tried until the bitter end to hold the relationship together, hating the prospect of being single and a single parent. I allowed my husband to intimidate me, so by the time he left, I felt unworthy to be loved by anyone. My 10-year-old daughter took on the burden of supporting me, and then when she was 16, she fell prey to drugs. She survived her bout with drugs and now is happy, with a family of her own.

—Barbara

A friend of mine was divorced with two small children, and she hurt very badly. She couldn't seem to get her life together. Her children were "driving her mad," so a dear friend gave her a trip away from the children for a few days. But because of the hurt and vulnerability she was experiencing at the time, she became involved with a man who said and did all the right things to cause her to fall in love with him. He showed her lots of attention and seemed to want to be a part of her and her children's lives. "The rest of the story," as Paul Harvey says, was that she married him, and then she found out that he was being unfaithful to her. He started abusing her children, and she had to leave him.

The shame, guilt, and humiliation that come with that kind of abuse lasts a long time, but I feel that when people make mistakes, they should understand what the mistake is, ask for forgiveness, and accept the forgiveness God offers. It is difficult for some of us to accept the forgiveness of the Lord or of others because we think we've been so stupid or ignorant in making such a mistake. We're afraid, particularly when we are hurting so badly, because we never know what other people's intentions are. I want to encourage you to keep in touch with friends who can give you advice and keep you accountable. You don't always have to take the advice that people give you, but if you ask somebody for advice, you need to listen.

Divorce is a traumatic event for children. In recent studies, psychologist Judith Wallerstein found that many years after their parents' divorce, adult children are suffering consequences such as worry, underachievement, self-deprecation, and anger. Two thirds of the girls involved in the study had sailed through their parents' divorces, but suddenly became anxious as young adults, fearful of betrayal by their mate and unable to make lasting commitments. Many of the boys, when grown, lacked a sense of independence and purpose, drifting from job to job and in and out of college. Experts seem to agree that children need to maintain a relationship with the parent who does not have custody, with a regular visitation schedule if possible. The children, for the most part, also feel more secure if they spend time with grandparents.

The most important factor in how well the children adapt seems to be the parents' attitudes toward each other. Sometimes divorce ends the fighting, but in some families, the fighting escalates. Letting go of the anger is one of the best things parents can do to help the children adjust. We can make a choice to walk in peace and forgiveness—for our children's sakes and also for our own peace of mind.

I believe one of the best ways God can heal broken hearts is through people in the church. All of us need a circle of friends who pray for us and encourage us. The church plays an integral part in this. I know that for me—through the tough times and the good times—it was the church family that held me up. The Bible says that we are commanded to love, to help, and to strengthen, as well as hold each other accountable. The New Testament repeatedly exhorts us to minister healing to each other on all levels—spiritual, emotional, and physical.

The Bible says we need to help the hurting ones—young or old, married or single—lift them up, and encourage them. Loving one another is the manifestation of the grace of God. It is easy to love the lovely, the ones who smell good and act nice, but we are challenged to love, accept, and encourage the ones who don't act right, smell right, dress right, or talk right. Just because we are different does not mean we are necessarily wrong. Different is different.

Chapter 5

Not Guilty—Some Things Are Not Your Fault

Rod McKuen, well-loved poet of the twentieth century, made a decision recently to share with others the tragic incident of sexual abuse that shook his childhood world. "The fact that my stepfather had beaten me up when I was a kid wasn't hard for me to talk or write about. I had both arms broken and my ribs caved in several times, but physical injuries on the outside heal. Before now, though, I have never been able to come forward and talk about having been sexually abused when I was a child. Those scars have never healed, and I expect they never will."

McKuen said that his stepfather's sister began to fondle him until he protested and ran away, and then, on a hunting trip with this woman's husband—whom he loved and trusted—the man sodomized him. "All the good things and all the wonderful times we had had together were gone, and I kept thinking to myself, 'What did I do to make him turn against me, to make him hate me so much that he would do this to me?' " The next day, Rod confronted the man and threatened to tell the entire neighborhood about the incident if he ever came near him again. He saw the couple only twice after that, but he couldn't shake the memory of those terrible episodes. "All of my life I have felt that somehow I did something to bring [the molestation] on. I don't know how to get rid of that feeling. Now, since I told my story, I'm beginning to believe there was nothing I could have done."

He's right—there is nothing he could have done. It was not his fault. It was the fault of an adult who took advantage of a child's trust. In fact, McKuen did the right thing by standing up to the man. If he hadn't, the abuse could have gone on for years. His story is a classic example of how we are made to feel guilty for things that happened to us in our childhood. This feeling of guilt is called *false guilt*, and we need to face it down with truth. The truth is that children aren't responsible for what is done to them. *Guilt* is defined as the fact of being responsible for an offense or wrongdoing. False guilt is many times used by the perpetrator as a tool to keep the child from telling anyone about the offense. The abuser somehow convinces the victim that he or she is responsible for the offense. This method of control is so successful that the false guilt stays on into adulthood, often affecting self-image and relationships.

Many of us have been robbed of joy and happiness in our lives because we have continued to carry the burden of false guilt. Left unresolved, the pressure of guilt can lead to serious physical, emotional, and spiritual problems.

In our relationships—especially family ones—we often take on self-reproach that stems from false guilt. Following are some of the guilt trips that we take on:

- *Obligation*. This is the false guilt trip designed to make the receiver feel responsible for something, thus feeling guilt if there is not an appropriate response. The way this guilt trip is designed, you can never win. You cannot win because even if you decide to respond to the guilt trip, you have to respond according to how the receiver wants that response to be. So you can keep trying to do the right thing, but may possibly never be able to successfully make it happen.

- *It's your fault* .The threat of this false guilt trip is that if something goes badly for someone else, it will be your fault. The hidden message here is that you will be shunned by the family for a period of time. No one wants that, of course, so it is easy to respond to this guilt trip in order to avoid getting emotionally hurt by family and friends.

- *Shame on you* .This guilt trip is threatening because it makes the quiet yet subtle statement that you are not a good person and have done something really bad—so bad that if you are not careful and do not stay under control of the family way of doing things, the family will reject you emotionally and, sometimes, physically.

- *Manipulation.* In this guilt trip, a family member uses guilt to motivate you to do what he or she wants you to do. For example, "You will really break your Mother's heart if you don't go to the birthday party that she has planned for you." There is no room for discussion. There is no room for acknowledgment that Mother was inappropriate in planning the birthday without your permission. You are just set up and are expected to cooperate. And most important, you get the message that you don't hurt anyone else, for any reason.

- *Threat of being embarrassed or disclosed.* This is another guilt trip that subtly says that you have done something so bad that if you get out of line you will be disclosed. This disclosure can be simply to the family or it can be shared with other people outside the family. This is such a powerful tool that families can keep control of their members with this ongoing, quiet threat.

I am a child of God, and God don't make no junk.

Ethel Waters

Not Guilty—Some Things Are Not Your Fault

How do these guilt trips get into our lives? Psychologists have, for years, tried to understand these painful styles and have finally determined that these guilt trips usually begin in the home.

Jan was sexually abused by her step-grandfather when she was small, and she is still haunted by the memory of his face. She said, "I can't deal with him as far as talking to him because he is dead now, but I want to deal with my feelings and what I've gone through. I want to be rid of that dirty feeling and insecurity. Most of all, I want to be rid of the guilt I have carried for years. That's been the worst problem I've had. The guilt spills over into every relationship I have. It's hard to trust God even though I know deep down that I can trust Him completely."

Jan's false guilt from something that was done *to* her has tainted all her relationships, even her relationship with God. That same kind of guilt affects every abuse victim, yet it's not their fault. No matter where the false guilt comes from, we need to protect ourselves from it and forgive ourselves in the case of any real guilt from the past. We may say, "I know God has forgiven me, but I don't feel forgiven." *Being* forgiven has nothing to do with *feeling* forgiven. Being forgiven is what God did for us and continues to do for us daily.

We don't have to remain prisoners of guilt, but in order to escape, we have to move forward with a decision to do something about it. We must reprogram our minds so that we can be released from the despair of false guilt. Up until this point, our minds have been programmed with old negative thoughts and haunting memories that we keep playing over and over again. When a negative message occurs, replace it with a positive one. For example, the statement I'm no good" can be replaced with a favorite statement of the late Ethel Waters, singer and entertainer, "I am a child of God, and God don't make no junk."

You can stop playing those old guilt tapes and replace them with positive statements. Here are some examples:

- Replace *You're no good* with *I'm a child of God.*

- Replace *You're so stupid* with *I am bright.*

- Replace *You're ugly* with *I am beautiful.*

- Replace *You're good for nothing* with *I have worth.*

- Replace *You are so selfish* with *I am kind.*

- Replace *I have to please everyone* with *I want to please God.*

The bottom line is that we don't have to remain in this terrible condition of guilt and shame. God's unconditional love is available to take care of these problems—it's up to us to respond and accept His unconditional love.

It is important that we recognize the hurt and move on. With patience and the Word of God, we can begin to change our thought patterns. As we focus on Christ and who we are in Him, we can be set free from guilt and shame from the past. Remember, the value of a $100 bill is the same even after it's been muddied, kicked, and wrinkled. You are valuable to God—just as valuable as the day you were born and just as valuable as the noblest person He has created.

Maybe you've been filled with guilt and shame because of the past. A constant or consistent feeling of shame can cause you to hate yourself, think that others do not like you, keep you from receiving compliments, and prevent you from believing people when they say they love you. I believe God is saying to you through this book that it's time to stop hating yourself and begin really accepting and loving yourself. Begin to believe the best—that you are loved—and when you are complimented, simply look the person in the eye and say, "Thank you."

There are four steps we can take to deal with false guilt. It's not necessarily an easy process, but it can be done.

1. Establish effective boundaries.

2. Begin to change patterns of thought and behavior one day at a time.

3. Communicate—confront, if needed.

4. Continue relationships, if possible, maintaining strong, healthy boundaries.

We can continue to win over guilt feelings when we establish priorities in our lives, especially making our relationship with God our top priority. Our thoughts and time need to be filled with God if we really want to lose the guilt trip. We live in the world, but we must set our minds on things above—especially if we want to be set free from the burden of guilt.

Chapter 6

Is a Diamond Found in a Sewer Less Valuable?

A healthy self-image is a basic foundation stone upon which we build success. People with healthy self-esteem like who they are and don't want to be anybody else. It took me a long time to understand this. People with a healthy self-image accept their faults, weaknesses, and strengths and are comfortable with themselves. No one around me expected me to attend college or to amount to much of anything. But I wanted something more but didn't know what. Why I wanted more is not really a question I could answer—except that I felt it was God's will for me, and I yielded to Him.

How I saw myself as a child

For many reasons—some good and some bad—I felt I was different. I had a vision that came from beyond my background. I wanted to be a better person. People did not encourage me; and few ever said to me, "I believe in you, and I believe you can make it" or "I'll take up for you" or "You are bright." I developed a poor self-image because of the poverty and sexual and verbal abuse that I experienced. Because of this, I became extremely depressed, and that's part of what caused me to make some wrong decisions along the way—decisions that caused hurt and pain. My journey of personal image was one of distorted ideas. As a child, I saw myself completely different than how others saw me. I felt ugly, shy, incapable, and beaten down. My hope is that through sharing my journey, others will learn at an earlier age and realize that even if we are not given much hope or if we mess up, we can still live good, productive, successful lives.

My perception of the world was limited to what I observed in my hometown. I was labeled early in life as "one of those poor Darlington kids." I not only felt it, but I was reminded of this several years ago when I went into a shop in Quitmore, Georgia, to buy something. The clerk remembered me and made a remark about my not being able to afford a particular item. Her perception of Mamie Claire was that I was only fit for "birthin' young'uns and cannin' tomatoes." I was fortunate to outdistance my label, but I wonder how many other people haven't been so lucky. You see, I was waving for help many times when I really felt hopeless and depressed and didn't even want anyone to save me. At one time, I broke out in welts, and there was no explanation or reason for it. Looking back, I believe my body was waving for help and I didn't even know it.

Labeling is dangerous. If we label anyone a bully or a clown or a dummy or a wallflower, or if we label someone fat or lazy, in time, he or she will become convinced that that is his or her real identity. We tend to believe what we are told about ourselves. Many times we become what we have been labeled by others. Used in a positive way, this can be a wonderful motivation, but used in a negative way, it can stifle a person's potential, which is a frightening thought. I often say when I speak, "As we see people, we treat them; as we treat them, oftentimes they become." In college, I was seen as I should be rather than as I was, and I blossomed with the help of some wonderful people. As parents, educators, and business leaders, we need to be more concerned about the people we are responsible for, especially the children. We need to see them as God sees them—"fearfully and wonderfully made."

Let me just say this: God never makes a mistake. If you're here, God made you, and since He made you, that means He made you for a purpose. You are His precious child, and that's a fact. Please believe that. Also, as long as you are on this earth, there is something you can do to brighten others' lives.

Why do we not use our talents and abilities? Why do we get involved in drugs, tobacco, or alcohol? Why do we want to be self-destructive? Why do we never start because we always feel inadequate? Why do we never live up to our potential? Why do we fail to finish a project? Why do we have the I-can't attitude about life? Why do we always look for a better deal? Why do we never seem to get along with peers?

Why? Because we have developed a low self-esteem or a poor self-image or, as I was saddled with early in life, an inferiority complex. We have been falsely identified or have a mistaken identity. When my son Brian was in high school, he was mistakenly identified by a witness as a Christmas light vandal. The real vandal was tall, wore glasses, and had a shiny jacket—just like Brian. When a policeman came to my door late one night, he said that Brian had been positively identified. When I asked who identified him, the officer said he could not tell me, but that Brian would be prosecuted for the crime. I insisted that the person who had identified Brian face him and tell me he was the one. As I prepared to go down to the police station, I thought about what I should wear. After all, I was sure the *Dallas Morning News* would carry the news with the headline MOTIVATIONAL SPEAKER'S SON JAILED. (I pictured what I would look like on the front page, so I decided to at least wear something that made me look thin.) Brian was quite upset and repeatedly said, "Mama, I did not do it." We drove to the home that had been vandalized, and when we met the owner, we asked if he recognized Brian as the vandal. The man replied, "No, I've never seen

"Bee" all that God wants you to be.

this young man before." Someone had connected the man's description of the culprit with Brian, and it resulted in a false arrest. Do not allow others to falsely identify you.

There are things we can do on a daily basis to develop a positive approach toward "growing" a healthy self-image. You will never hear me say "better than," but I want you to *bee* the best you can be, using your talents and abilities to become all you are meant to be. When we plant a tomato seed, tomatoes come up. When we plant a negative thought, negative thoughts come out. When we plant negative self-image we reap negative self-image. Positive input produces positive results.

As we imagine ourselves to be, so in time, we will become

I had heard this quote many times in my life and tried to visualize my life in ten, fifteen, and twenty years. I frankly had trouble doing this—so I decided to practice telling the truth in advance.

In 1983 we completed a multimillion-dollar building program at our church in Dallas, Texas. The big dedication day came and we were all so excited because a large number of prominent people were going to be in the service that day. My phone rang early that Sunday morning. It was my pastor. "Mamie," he said, "we are having a group for lunch today at Bent Tree Country Club, and we would like to have you join us." Naturally I said yes, because I had always wanted to visit Bent Tree Country Club. I had no idea who would be attending, but I was too busy to think about that. I had to get the children to church and taken care of so that I could attend the luncheon.

I arrived at Bent Tree after all the other guests had arrived, thank goodness. I pulled up to the valet service in my mud-speckled car with my Bible, the children's Sunday-school pictures, and drink cans overflowing onto the floorboard. I quickly tried to tidy the car up and left the keys with the parking attendant. I went into the beautiful building and asked where the luncheon was being held. Everyone was very cordial and gave me prompt directions. Being the last one to arrive, I had a choice of one seat—between Mary Kay Ash of Mary Kay Cosmetics and George Beverly Shea of the Billy Graham Crusade. Across the table was Judge Abner McCall of Baylor University, and all the other guests were just as impressive. When the luncheon was over and I was driving home, I realized that I had been in "tall cotton" that day, and I felt good and comfortable about it. My car was a several-years'-old station wagon and my suit was one of my Nelly New from a resale shop. None of that bothered me, however, and I realized for the first time that I felt good about being Mamie McCullough, a single widow with three children to raise. I had not allowed anyone to make me feel inferior. I suppose for the first time that I truly believed the statement that Eleanor Roosevelt made, "No one can make you feel inferior without your permission." Oh, what a relief it is. A good, healthy self-image is acquired through many steps, processes, and determination to *bee* all that God wants you to be. This is an ongoing process.

Self-worth and self-esteem are like having 100 chances on a new car as opposed to 5 chances. The more chances you have, the more likely you are to win. The more we understand and realize our talent, and the more we risk trying—walking by faith, not by sight—the more reserve we have. It takes understanding, education, and love. With this reserve of strength, it takes more to get us down. When we broaden our education, our attitudes, and our resources, we have more choices and greater reserves in all areas.

Self-image is a system of pictures and feelings that we have constructed about ourselves at the heart of our personality—"As a man thinketh in his heart, so is he" (Proverbs 23:7 KJV). I reiterate—not better than anyone else, but the best you can be to develop, serve, and live.

We hear, read, and talk a great deal about self-image or self-esteem. The fashion world, toothpaste advertisements, exercise equipment, and, yes, some people tell us if we do certain things, live in a certain area of town, drive a certain type of car, wear a certain brand of watch, jewelry, or clothes, or are seen at special places, we'll all feel good about ourselves. Are these people right? Well, we want to believe that this is true, but we are only prolonging the real answer. Good self-image is a process of doing your best each day.

Even before you were born, your being was formed by your genes, your parents, and many other factors that make you an individual. However, you are the only one among the 6.5 billion people on this earth with your particular thumbprint. I like to say, "You are thumbody." You are the only one with your talents, abilities, dreams, and experiences—and only you can decide how you will use them.

We never know how people perceive themselves. As I begin many of my more than 100 speeches a year to corporate groups, churches, and schools, I say, "This is the best day of my life, and no one has ever felt as good as I do today despite what I have been through."

The abuse I suffered at the hands of family friends was by far the worst thing that could have ever happened to my self-esteem. I was afraid and ashamed, and I felt guilty just for being alive. Men from church as well as men who didn't attend church managed to manipulate me into uncomfortable situations that as a child I had no way of avoiding. The abuse was so well hidden that my family never suspected it. After my horrible experiences from age five to age nine, I did not know what to do about them, and I held my head low. I didn't talk when attention was focused on me because when I did, I broke out in welts all over my body. I didn't answer any questions. I felt dirty, sinful, shameful, and ugly. I hated the people involved, and I hated myself. In my mind I was a bad girl. Anger was building inside me, but I couldn't share it because I felt no one would believe me. Only bad girls got involved in nasty things like that, I thought. I wanted to forget the whole thing, but that was impossible. The images of what happened haunted my memory. I wanted to be anybody but me. It never occurred to me to tell anyone. Looking back, it might have been a blessing that I did not tell. Many people who *did* tell were hospitalized for mental disorders, and some are still hostages today. It took years for me to overcome the impact of child abuse on my already negative self-image.

One cause of a poor self-image is comparing oneself to others, as I did. This is always harmful. We don't need to be in competition with anyone else. As I learned years later, success is not measured by how we compare with others. Success is measured by comparing our accomplishments to our capabilities and being able to live up to our potential. I encourage you to strive to be the very best you that you can become.

Yes, you can, and I can too.

A good self-image is not an egotistical I'm-better-than-you attitude. It's simply becoming the best that you can possibly be and doing what needs to be done at the time. If you get up in the morning, look in the mirror, and see a "nobody," you feel you're hopeless and have nothing to offer. Often you don't try your best because you don't feel you deserve the good things in life: a good marriage, beautiful and healthy children, a steady job, a nice home, or a nice car. I was guilty of feeling like a zero on a scale of one-to-ten for years. Then I read Zig Ziglar's *See You at the Top*, and learned I could be closer to a ten with some changes, goals, and determination. During the last thirty years, I've been writing about and teaching the I Can way of life to help others, and I've discovered that I don't have to feel second class because of the things that happened to me years ago. The abusers were the guilty ones, not me. It's important to acknowledge that the perpetrator is the guilty one and not the one who was abused. The abusing adults are the ones who did wrong, not the innocent children.

An important part of being you and maintaining a good self-image is learning to say no. Many of us enjoy pleasing others, but if we go to the extreme to please others, we have really hurt everyone involved. If I take on too many speaking engagements, and I'm not rested enough to do my best, then I've let everyone down, including myself. Nobody wins unless I know to say no. People with a healthy self-image learn to say no at the proper time to build boundaries. As a child, I was too shy, timid, and hurt to express my feelings and to say no to the perpetrators. Teach your family to say no when it affects their space.

Please remember that almost everyone has moments of self-doubt. There are still times when my childhood traumas and self-doubts sneak into my mind. If this happens to you, fight back. Don't allow those concepts to pervade your thoughts and actions. Instead, learn to replace the negative by filling your mind with good, positive thoughts. This comes from reading good books, listening to inspirational tapes and music, attending good seminars, staying physically fit, and spending time with loving and supportive friends. I encourage you to be yourself—your best self, but yourself. You have suffered enough from "malnutrition of your youth"—this means that because you did not have the emotional, physical, and safety support you needed as a child, your soul was not fed and nurtured as it should have been.

These are some of the feelings I had from childhood. I felt like a nobody from nowhere, and I felt like I was not smart because of my family. I was depressed and thought I didn't deserve anything good, and I did not want to live. I was convinced that I was not capable and that I would never be financially free. I felt overweight, fat, and out of shape. I was overly sensitive and felt guilty from the past wrongs. I felt hurt because of some of the decisions I had made, and I suffered from claustrophobia.

The good news is that you may not have all of these manifestations of a poor self-image, but some of them may become apparent to you. In all honesty, I've felt most of these. I've been angry, fearful, and anxious. I was shy, unmotivated, irritable, and fault-finding of others. I wanted to control others, suffered from a broken spirit and poor concentration, and I felt lonely.

Much of my memory has been blocked, and I have felt incompetent and unable to handle rejection. I have had numerous physical ailments and sleeping disorders, and I have felt hopeless. At times I've made poor choices because of wrong priorities, and I have been sorely tempted to rebel against authority. Many times I suffer from flashbacks of the past abuse because of certain people, places, and smells. I made a decision, though, that life is too short to remain in the trap of poor self-esteem.

There are some specific ways you can improve your self-image. You can start by being willing to change. You can be yourself—the best you that you can be—without comparing yourself to others. You can choose to stop negatively labeling yourself and others. You can be a people-builder, instead. Surround yourself with good friends who encourage you, pray for you, and lift your spirits. Try making your own personal "victory list." Write down your victories, no matter how small, and regularly review the good things you've done.

We can work to achieve healthy attitudes by being kind, caring, and compassionate. We can choose to be happy and friendly, to deal honestly with others, and to take good care of our bodies. Let's forgive and move on, accepting ourselves and others as we are. I encourage you to look for the best in others rather than being critical. We should be happy when others are successful. Then, when we are self-directed and unafraid to take risks, we will be able to effectively use our talents and become content with life as it is lived. We become better, not bitter, and we enjoy peace of mind. We can be happy and able to laugh with others. This is what I call an I Can attitude toward life.

There are some practical things we can do to gain and maintain a positive self-image. We can begin by getting rid of our blame list. Then we need to accept the facts of life: work, career, children or no children. We will be much happier when we replace worry with prayer and Bible study, when we learn to value life, and when we take the time to rest. Never make a major decision when you are too tired to make it. Rest first, and then evaluate the situation.

Making friends at church, work, clubs, and in your neighborhood will greatly improve your outlook on life. Never forget to lighten up, laugh, and be happy.

If you've been inactive, this is the time to change that. Get physically fit with exercise and healthy eating. Thirty minutes a day of walking for four days a week will keep you healthy—physically and mentally. Fix what you can about your appearance. Yes, I had some plastic surgery to improve my nose in 1965. I always say, "One more face-lift and they'll have to do it by Caesarean."

Do something nice for someone who cannot return the favor. Visit the home of a senior citizen. Give a friend something of yours that she likes. Write a note to others who serve—teachers, clergy, mail carrier, garbage collector. Get involved and volunteer in mission work: homeless, halfway house, community programs, soup kitchen, or abused women and children.

This is a time when you can make memories with your friends and family, remembering the good times. Make a dream sheet—apply WD-40 to your dream machine. Begin processing the hurt by writing a letter to the offender. Plan a retreat for yourself, a friend, or friends. Read good, positive books, including the Bible.

Do something you loved as a child, like fly a kite, chase a butterfly, or go barefoot in a stream. Play on a park swing, eat an ice-cream cone, play a game of cards or kickball, make a mud pie, or pick wildflowers. Maybe you could plant some flowers, sit on a creek bank and skip stones, or listen to nature.

Find a mentor, someone to look up to, an example. Maintain a support system of people who encourage you. Learn how to honor and bless others. Be consistent in tasks. Set aside a special time each day for Bible reading and prayer. Attend church or synagogue regularly. Find a good prayer partner.

You might try doing things that are hard for you early in the day when you are fresh. Get up, make up, dress up. It doesn't take a lot of money to look your best. Do your best to be clean and neat. Smile and be kind, courteous, and gracious.

Choose friends carefully. Associate with people of high moral character. Start now. Just do it. Learn to respond rather than to react. Understand who you are in Christ. Cultivate your talent(s): singing, playing piano, drawing, writing, decorating, sewing, cooking. Build your own self up by living as a good role model. Write down things to do each day. Doing this the night before is very effective. Remember, it takes time and love. Lead with love.

It's okay to get help from a counselor or valued friend. Keep learning and doing—"grow through life." Try new things. Paint, skydive, scuba dive. See yourself as a success and a winner. Imagine it.

You may want to evaluate your habits and attitudes and make a never-again list. Don't give up, keep trying. Learn to finish jobs. As someone said, "Do it right the first time." As it was explained to me, if you don't have time to do it right the first time, how will you ever find time to redo it?

> When a task is once begun,
> Leave it not until it's done.
> Be a matter great or small,
> Do it well or not at all.

Learn some manners. Check out a book from the library and tune up your social skills. Develop open communication with others. Listen with silence. Listening is loving. Remember, success in life and a healthy positive self-image come from our attempt to find meaning and purpose totally dependent on God. We are created in His likeness. We were created by God to be in His image, like Him, and filled with His power.

Confess your sins. Confession is good for the soul. In recovery from an addiction, acknowledgment of the problem is an act of trust. Trusting thoughts and behavior can promote beneficial effects. Learn to stop destructive thoughts. Mentally stop yourself from demeaning yourself or others. Treat each day as though it were your last. Talk and share with people you trust and admire. Learn to laugh at yourself when you do something foolish. Terminate relationships that are negative and drag you down. In other words, end uncaring friendships.

Let others know how much you appreciate them. Keep a Happy Box filled with cards, notes, pictures, and remembrances from friends and family. As my friend Diane Tate says, "We need a happy." Apologize for unkept promises with a letter or phone call. Realize all decisions are not the same. Try to avoid high-maintenance people. They pull too much from us. Say positive words, such as *You can* or *I believe in you.*

Remember: God provides us a way through a situation but not out of it. He is our Comforter in hard times. He gives us the peace and returns our joy. Mother Teresa said, "Give the best you can." Get organized. Learn to listen. Learn to negotiate. According to Chester Karrass, *"You do not get what you deserve. You get what you negotiate."*

Get yourself together. Decide who you are and learn to communicate this to others. Do not be judgmental. You cannot have a healthy inner self unless you have the guts to stand on your own two feet, think for yourself, and grow. If all you have is a developed bitter self, all you'll have is a product like some films—overexposed and underdeveloped. The more you grow as a person, the less shocked you become about people who are different from yourself. I encourage you to understand and accept the fact that we all have different tastes and opinions. Different is not all bad. "Far out," however, does not leave us much room to give a good impression.

Matthew Arnold said, "The same heart beats in every human breast."

There's a popular children's poem by Shel Silverstein in his book *Where the Sidewalk Ends,* entitled "Sick". It gives thirty-nine excuses—from measles to heart trouble—for not wanting to get out of bed, until the child in the poem finally discovered it was not a school day, but Saturday. The response of the child changed from sickness to, "I'm going out to play." Much like the child in the poem, we often look for ways to escape our responsibility, but it is important for us to keep our commitments. Doing what we're committed to with our work, home, family, and friends is basic to our journey as a child of the King.

We do not have to feel good to be good

Others—even our best friends—cannot shut down our worst fears and deepest agonies. Others never fully understand the battle some of us face or the words inflicted on us. Only through a deep abiding faith in God can we understand and begin to accept and process hurts, fears, and disappointments.

We must understand that there isn't a one-time cure-all, solution. Life is a walk, a process, a journey, a growing time. We've all heard the saying that time heals everything. But that's not true. Often we are hurting so badly that it's just as bad to be reminded of the pain, and it's often magnified. We must realize that life will always have hurt. Hurt is no respecter of age, race, size, or personality. None of us was ever promised a painless, easy way of life, but the shortcut to healing the pain, the hurt, and the depression is knowledge.

I have served on a board here in Dallas for dropout kids, youth who often have been abandoned and have had to learn on the streets. They have been told that they are nothing and can do nothing. One young man told me about his life with no family and no encouragement. He told me he had stolen, lied, and cheated all his life. He said, "No one ever told me I had anything to give, so I took."

We all have something to give, including you. You have something to give, and you have talents and abilities. I want to encourage you to see yourself as the real you—the valuable you. You were brought into this world for a reason—to be everything God made you to be.

Positive image—positive imagination

Imagination rules the world. Nothing is discovered or invented without imagination. It is the preview of life's coming attractions. Again, "As you imagine yourself to be, so in time you will become." All successful people actively pursue developing a healthy self-image. Successful athletes see themselves winning. Tiger Woods, the golfer, has Jack Nicholas's golfing record posted on his wall, and he looks at it every day. I'm sure he imagines a picture of himself beating that record every time he walks onto a golf course. His images become his possession. We have heard the cliché, What you see is what you get. Woods is proving that saying to be true. See yourself winning, and you will play with that kind of skill. We must all face who and what we really are in life.

Chapter 7

Dealing with Anger and Fear

Anger weakens a man. It puts him at a disadvantage in every undertaking in life. When Sinbad and his sailors landed on a tropical island, they saw high up in the trees, coconuts that could quench their thirst and satisfy their hunger. The coconuts were far above the reach of Sinbad and the sailors, but in the branches of the trees were the chattering apes. Sinbad and his men began to throw stones and sticks up at the apes. This enraged the monkeys, and they began to seize the coconuts and hurl them down at the men on the ground. That was just what Sinbad and his men wanted. They got the apes angry so that they would gather their food for them. This is a good illustration of how by indulging in anger, we play into the hands of our foes.

—C. E. Macartney

Anger

Psychologist Charles Spielberger defines anger as an emotional state that varies in intensity from mild irritation to intense fury and rage. When we get angry, our heart rate and blood pressure rise, along with our levels of adrenaline. Anger comes from external and internal causes, and it is a natural response to threats. It is a completely normal human emotion, but when it gets out of control and becomes destructive, it can cause problems.

Anger keeps us from evaluating a situation objectively, causes us to hold on to hate, envy, and jealousy, and keeps us prisoners of our own wrath. It is mentally unhealthy when we hold in our anger, and it often results in bitterness, hostility, poor self-esteem, relationship problems, eating disorders, phobias, and self-doubt.

Here are some biblical ways to handle inappropriate anger:

- Seek out the source of your anger. "Search me, O God, and know my heart; test me and know my anxious thoughts. See if there is any offensive way in me, and lead me in the way everlasting" (Psalm 139:23–24 NIV).

- Give your anger to God. "Cast all your anxiety on him because he cares for you" (1 Peter 5:7).

- Pray for those who persecute you. Jesus said, "Love your enemies and pray for those who persecute you" (Matthew 5:44).

- Forgive as the Lord forgave you. "Bear with each other and forgive whatever grievances you may have against one another. Forgive as the Lord forgave you" (Colossians 3:13).

- Trust God to bring good from your trials. "We know that in all things God works for the good of those who love him, who have been called according to his purpose" (Romans 8:28).

Some people go around angry all the time without any apparent reason. Some of the most common causes for this include:

1. *Dissatisfaction with self.* Feelings of low self-esteem may come from having felt unloved or having been physically, mentally, or sexually abused as children. Studies show that children who have experienced such abuse grow up filled with feelings of chronic anger, and they often abuse their own children or spouses or commit acts of violence toward other

people. It's important to get into psychological counseling in order to break the cycle of violence that otherwise would be passed on from generation to generation. Most men who suffer from chronic low self-esteem usually feel that they have to keep proving their manhood. To make up for their feelings of inadequacy, they are driven to always win. They are poor losers and feel threatened if they are losing even in a friendly game. They tend to drive aggressively and recklessly, get furious if anyone passes them or cuts them off, and often react with violent behavior even to minor upsets.

2. *Perfectionism.* Many people tend to be perfectionists, unable to deal with their own inadequacies or those of others. They go through life with a perpetual chip on their shoulder, making themselves and those around them miserable.

3. *Chronic fatigue.* When people get very tired, their ability to cope with everyday problems of living decreases, and they become extremely irritable, lashing out at everyone around them for no apparent reason.

4. *Physical illness.* Physical illness may have the same effect because one simply doesn't have the energy to cope with ordinary problems that could usually be handled. The best thing to do in this case is explain feeling unwell and ask that others be patient with.

5. *Mental illness.* This is sometimes expressed by unprovoked anger or irritation. The mentally ill sometimes feel that everyone is persecuting or mistreating them.

6. *Depression.* This makes people mean and short-tempered, even with those who are trying hard to please. When appropriately diagnosed in treatment, depression can be greatly alleviated.

7. *Drug and alcohol abuse.* This affects the ability to cope with ordinary events in one's life and completely changes the user's behavior.

Regardless of what degree of anger is manifesting in your life, there is hope. There are several healthy ways of dealing with anger. Most of us have been trained from early childhood to suppress anger, but we really need to learn how to appropriately express it by admitting our anger verbally. This is like releasing steam from a pressure cooker.

Don't deny your anger, but express it in constructive and effective ways, such as a few well-chosen words to make the point. It's important to keep your anger from destructive action of any kind. Expressing your anger rationally can be useful when it leads to constructive dialogue. It's important to get your anger out in the light.

I was angry at my friend,
I told my wrath, my wrath did end.
I was angry at my foe,
I told it not, my wrath did grow.

Here are four strategies for dealing with anger:

1. Breathe deeply from your diaphragm.

2. Slowly repeat a calming phrase such as "Take it easy" or "Just relax."

3. Visualize a relaxing experience from your memory.

4. Do stretching, muscle-relaxing exercises.

The best thing to do about anger is to change the way you think. Replace overly dramatic, irrational thoughts like "It's terrible! Everything is ruined!" with more rational thoughts like "It's frustrating, but it's not the end of the world. Losing my temper won't help the situation at all." Yelling, using words like *never* and *always*, or cursing not only cause problems with others, but they also tend to increase your anger. Remind yourself that the world is not out to get you. Make yourself slow down and carefully think through your responses. Give yourself a break; remove yourself from your immediate surroundings if feasible. If you feel that your anger is really out of control, consider getting counseling. You can't eliminate anger from your life, but you can certainly change the way anger affects you.

Fear

As I mentioned earlier, when my children were small, I experienced acute claustrophobia (a fear of confined spaces) for the first time at a teacher's convention in 1976, and until 1980, I could not sleep in a hotel room above the first floor. My claustrophobia became so bad, that, as I continued to travel, I had to spend most of the nights in the lobby of the hotel rather than in my room.

When I tell about these experiences, some of my listeners ask how I handled this fear, trapped inside a closed-up airplane while flying to my speaking engagements. That was a different matter. I didn't have a choice. When the doors had been secured, I knew I couldn't open a window or door to relieve my tensions. I just gritted my teeth and accepted the reality that I had no choice in this matter. I then stayed busy reading, listening to tapes, or visiting with seatmates. It was not easy, but we do what we have to do. Many of us look at our fears and think they cannot be overcome, but I sincerely believe we can overcome them when we face them and understand that they are fears only and not reality.

If you are one of the thousands who have phobias, my advice to you is that you can overcome. The four years of trial-and-error study-and-prayer was something I did without counseling, as I was too busy raising children, working, teaching, and speaking to get outside help, not to mention the expense. However, I believe counseling is a great source of help. Whether this will work for you, I have no way of knowing, but

Fear is
False
Evidence
Appearing
Real

Zig Ziglar

I do know I travel about 100,000 miles a year and spend up to 175 days in hotels and motels with no problem (unless I find myself getting too tired and then I have to do self-talk.)

Earlier, I referred to the fact that I wanted you to feel safe in the arms of perhaps your mother or grandmother. You need to feel that someone cares enough to wipe your tears and reinforce your safety; you need the reassurance that repeated violations will never happen again. You need to be told that the harm that others have done to you will not happen again. Reinforcement is necessary. It diminishes the effect your childhood fears have on you today. I do not want you to live in fear. Perhaps if you did not have someone like this, then you may become that safety net for someone else.

As Susan, a twenty-five-year-old legal secretary, was leaving her office one night, she was suddenly struck with an overwhelming fear she had never experienced before. She felt as though something terrible was going to happen to her. She became flushed and almost couldn't catch her breath.

She tried to stay calm, but her fear just got worse and she became dizzy and lightheaded. She had no idea why. Finally she was able to make it outside for some fresh air, and gradually the fear subsided. Susan, like millions of others in our country alone, had suffered a panic attack. You and I have probably known people who have suffered these attacks. They are very real and can be debilitating.

Getting a grip on the panic

Panic has a way of battering our egos. We think we're freaks, panicking in the face of things that make most people yawn. Matthew Lambert, a psychologist at Texas Tech University, says to stop putting yourself down. He suggests these ways of coping with eight-legged friends and similar sources of terror:

- *Stay calm.* When you confront the source of your phobia, it's important to stay in control. Take even, deep breaths—hyperventilating only causes more anxiety.

- *Have a plan.* Don't jump around and yell. Follow through with a plan you've thought out beforehand, like smashing the spider or letting it wander.

- *Think positive.* Tell yourself that you're in command and that no matter what happens, you'll be okay. A sense of control is key, since fears prey on your feeling of powerlessness.

- *Consider getting help.* Your phobia can be overcome through familiarization techniques that can find success in three to six months. But don't go it alone. Seek out professional guidance through your local psychological association, your church, or friends. Ask for recommendations.

Fear is defined as an unpleasant emotional state, and a foreboding of an imagined or real state with physical symptoms such as shallow breathing, trembling, anxiousness, and mental confusion.

Make a positive statement as our President did on September 11, 2001:

"These acts shattered steel, but they cannot dent the steel of American resolve."

—President George W. Bush

On that September day, we all watched in shock, disbelief, anger, and resolution to what happened to change our world. As the World Trade Center buildings were destroyed—and so many lives were lost and families affected—both our country and our world were forever changed. A blanket of fear seemed to cover the country. Even as President George W. Bush told us to resume our daily lives and to not succumb to the fears that the enemy wanted us to give in to (to cause us to give up), many reacted in fear. I believe that since that tragic event, we have reevaluated our jobs, our homes, our families, and our spiritual lives. There was some good that came out of the September 11 tragedy. People are returning to the basics. Family seems more important, and people in general are more thankful for what they have. There is always a fear of repeated injustice, however. This is Satan's way of discouraging us and making us fearful and distrusting. When we surrender to fear, we are actually choosing to live as weaklings. Fears shroud and diminish our quality of life. Since 2001, we are evaluate and then putting forth our best to prove to ourselves that we can trust again.

In facing our fears, there is a right time to confront them. There is a documented story of how one person learned the mechanics of flying to help her get over her fear of flying. She climbed aboard an airplane for the first time in six years, a little apprehensive, but able to begin her journey to recovery.

What are the areas of fear in your life? Losing your job? Suffering? What's happening to our society? We're all afraid of something, but don't give up, because there is hope for overcoming your fears, and I believe you can do it. I encourage you to learn to face down your fears. Use the practical help you find in this chapter to find the courage to overcome.

Whether your fears are causing you a handicap or not, here are eight tips for facing them:

1. Remember to breathe deeply and slowly, causing you to remain calm.

2. Have something available to read or someone available to make conversation with.

3. Be careful of movies and television programs that feed your fears.

4. Learn to challenge your fears.

5. Write down your fears in detail. This will allow you to distinguish what is real and what is imagined.

6. Keep track of your progress.

7. Make a list of people to talk to about your fears. Choose three people—from friends, spiritual counselors, or a support team—and express your feelings and thoughts in detail.

8. Remember, it is mind over emotions.

Fear not, for I have redeemed you. Isaiah 43:1 (NIV)

The phrase *fear not*, is used 365 times in the Bible. We all have fears at different times in our lives, and they can become a handicap if we allow it. These fears occur in childhood—fears of being dropped, the darkness, animals, loud noises—to adulthood, when we fear the future, the weakening of our society, living insignificant lives, failing or being rejected, being sick, dying. After September 11, our society experienced fear of flying and of diseases such as anthrax. Even the daily routine of opening the mail became a fearful experience.

Fears have a way of crippling our daily lives if they go unprocessed. Unresolved fear results in anxiety disorders such as anger/rage, sadness/depression, and fear/anxiety. Fears are based on our life experiences, the environment, our resources (capabilities), our support system, and our perception of our ability to cope. An individual can turn fear and anxiety into a way of life by procrastinating—"If I run, I don't learn to manage my life." Let's face our fears. I believe admitting or expressing our fears begins the healing process.

What can we do to overcome our fears? Here are twelve ways:

1. Face the fear. Write it on paper.

2. Talk about your thoughts with friends or a counselor.

3. Change your mind about the reality of fear.

4. Consider this: "FEAR is False Evidence Appearing Real," Zig Ziglar.

5. Receive help from trained professionals.

6. Be willing to make some changes—and change detrimental old habits.

7. Monitor fearful thoughts, and substitute more rational responses to a situation.

8. Deal with anxieties immediately.

9. Learn to control fear rather than avoid it.

10. Learn to focus on the here and now and not on what might happen.

11. Seek professional medical treatment—perhaps a second opinion.

12. Use scripture affirmations to change your thinking. Use common sense.

Fear keeps us up all night, but faith makes one fine pillow.
—Philip Gulley

Chapter 8

Depression—Turn Your Hurt to Hope

My experience with depression has been one of ups and downs. As early as my teen years, I was overwhelmed by extended periods of self-doubt, emptiness, and feelings of being pressed down and rejected. I could not sleep; yet at other times I wanted to sleep. People can and do function in these times of depression, but no one would ever have believed that I suffered from depression and still do. I've had medication, taken many vitamins, and used preventive methods to help combat this disorder. I have found that exercise and a positive mental attitude are vital. Work is a blessing, not a punishment, because it has helped me to function and continue with my family and friends. Work, church, and my family have been my constant balance. You can live with depression, but I hope you will seek medical and psychological help to maintain a better quality of life.

Everyone gets sad sometimes—a brief mood, feelings of disappointment, or the more serious grief following the loss of a loved one. Depression is not a mere case of the blues; it's more than a period of sadness. Depression is a serious medical illness that affects

Don't give up and don't be afraid to ask for help.

the body as much as it does our moods and thoughts. To determine whether someone is suffering from depression, a doctor looks for at least five of the following nine symptoms that occur almost daily for two weeks.

1. feelings of sadness, depressed mood, irritability

2. loss of interest or pleasure in such activities as hobbies or family time

3. changes in weight or appetite

4. changes in sleeping pattern—sleeping too much or not at all

5. feelings of guilt, hopelessness, or worthlessness

6. inability to concentrate, remember things, or make decisions

7. constant fatigue or loss of energy

8. restlessness or decreased activity

9. recurrent thoughts of suicide or death

Depression is not something to be ashamed of. It is not a character flaw or a sign of weakness. People with depression can't just "snap out of it." It can be triggered by stress, medication, or physical illness. It can also be caused by an imbalance of certain chemicals in the brain.

According to the National Institute of Mental Health, more than 17 million Americans—one out of every ten people—develop depression each year. The good thing is that up to 80 percent of people who receive proper treatment for depression get better. Depression is treatable through appropriate medical intervention and support from loved ones.

Depression is just as real as a cut hand or broken bone, yet we usually feel uncomfortable about revealing our feelings of depression. There are times when it looks hopeless, and this is when we need to seek counseling from a professional. God has given those who help us the talents of encouragement, listening, and advice. When we need help, let's ask.

Depression is more than a feeling of temporary sadness. It is accompanied by a gloomy mind-set and usually causes mental dullness due to poor concentration and pessimistic thinking patterns. Depression can last a few hours, several months, or years. It is not one single isolated emotion; rather, it is a culmination of many negative feelings. To be depressed actually means to be pushed or pressed down. I've had people tell me they have never suffered depression; for me, however, this has been a reoccurring problem for over fifty years.

In addition to seeking professional counseling, here are twelve ways to deal with depression:

1. Examine yourself for a sense of self-confidence or a sense of well-being, which is contingent on *self-image*. *Self-esteem*, on the other hand, is based upon God's love for us. How do you see yourself?

2. Develop open communication. Seek openness in your relationships with others (the friendship factor). "Two are better than one" (Ecclesiastes 4:9 NIV). Those who are depressed tend to draw back from others or close them out. They've probably had negative experiences in their interpersonal relationships. It's important for us to learn to share needs, feelings, and aspirations with others. Likewise, it is important to be involved in their lives and needs as well.

3. Develop and stick with a plan of action, and have close friends for accountability purposes.

4. Be involved in a daily routine (including work, play, housework, projects) that brings personal satisfaction to you. Be convinced that your routine is God's will and purpose for your life. Put your all into each day.

5. Set aside time for God, including prayer and scripture study. Set aside time to pray and renew your mind.

6. Find time for personal mental health. You need time to unwind and relax. (Use tapes, books, or music.) Learn to relax.

7. Get rid of grudges. Forgive yourself for mistakes and forgive others for their errors.

8. Set aside enough time to be continually building a more intimate relationship with your mate. This includes time for fun, fellowship, serious communication, and a fulfilling sex life.

9. For couples, set aside time every week for date nights. If you are single, spend time with friends to relax and enjoy yourself.

10. Set aside time to adequately train your children; communicate your morals, values, and thoughts.

11. Do something nice for one special person each week. It can be physical (helping with chores), emotional (listening), or spiritual (praying or having devotions together).

12. Set aside a specific time four times a week for physical exercise, such as walking, jogging, or bicycling. The important thing is to keep moving.

> The problem is not the problem.
> The problem is
> my attitude about the problem.

The devil's best tool

It was announced that the devil was going out of business and would offer all his tools for sale to whoever would pay his price.

On the night of the sale they were all attractively displayed, and a bad looking lot they were. Malice, hatred, envy, jealousy, sensuality, deceit, and all the other implements of evil were spread out, each marked with its price. Apart from the rest lay a harmless-looking wedge-shaped tool, much worn and priced higher than any of them. Someone asked the devil what it was.

"That's discouragement," was the reply.

"Well, why do you have it priced so high?" he asked.

"Because," replied the devil, "it is more useful to me than any of the others. I can pry open and get inside a man's consciousness with that when I could not get near him with any of the others, and when once inside, I can use him in whatever way suits me best. It is so much worn because I use it with nearly everybody, as very few people yet know it belongs to me."

It hardly need be added that the devil's price for discouragement was so high that it was never sold. He still owns it and is still using it. Our best defense against a deceiving, lying devil is to simply believe God's Word and the precious promises it contains for us personally.

—Anonymous

The Lord is faithful, and he will strengthen
and protect you from the evil one.
2 Thessalonians 3:3 NIV

You will keep in perfect peace him whose mind is steadfast,
because he trusts in you.
Isaiah 26:3 NIV

These are God's promises to us concerning discouragement. We can't afford to entertain negative, discouraging thoughts. And we can't afford *not* to keep our minds and hearts on the Lord.

Researchers have isolated many causes of depression, including

- abuse

- pent-up anger

- loneliness

- lack of self-worth (inferiority complex)

- lack of intimacy with others

- lack of intimacy with God

In his book *Beating Depression* published by Facts On File, Dr. John Rush of the University of Texas Southwestern Medical Center gives a concise history of depression and cross-cultural prevalence, offers an in-depth look at how depression is diagnosed, describes the various types of depression and their causes, and discusses the methods of treatment available to the depressed person.

Depression is not only an adult disease, but it is also now common among youth. There have been diagnosed cases in children as young as four years old. Medication and psychological treatment are used at an early age. One in every thirty-three children and one in eight adolescents in this country have been diagnosed with depression, according to the National Mental Health Association. While depression in adults is widely recognized, depression in children is not.

Recognizing the problem

Depression is a form of mental illness that affects the way a person feels, thinks, and acts. Childhood depression, just as childhood abuses, if left untreated, can lead to school failure, alcohol or other drug use, and even suicide. Signs of childhood depression include:

- persistent sadness and hopelessness

- withdrawal from friends and activities once enjoyed

- increased irritability or agitation

- missed school or poor school habits

- indecision, lack of concentration, and forgetfulness

- poor self-esteem or guilt

- frequent physical complaints, such as headaches or stomachaches

- lack of enthusiasm, low energy or motivation

- drug or alcohol abuse

- recurring thoughts of death or suicide

Major depression, also known as *clinical* depression or *unipolar* depression, is only one type of a depressive disorder. Other depressive disorders include *dysthymia* (chronic, less severe depression) and *bipolar disorder* (manic depression). People who have bipolar disorder experience both depression and mania. *Mania* involves abnormally and persistently elevated mood or irritability, elevated self-esteem, and excessive energy, thoughts, and talking.

If you suffer from any form of depression, I encourage you to get medical help. Meanwhile, you can begin on the road to health by applying some of the practical suggestions in this chapter. Most important, don't give up. There is hope, and there is healing for you.

Chapter 9

Building Boundaries

Looking out from the window of an airplane as I'm flying each week, I'm always amazed at the world's topography—the mountains, cliffs, and valleys. What would happen if we had no lines or landmarks to show us where the boundaries are?

Boundaries help us recognize and change old false beliefs that would haunt us through adulthood and cause us to be closed to being creative. Old false beliefs cause us not to use our talents and abilities, therefore hindering our success.

Boundaries give us control and an action plan for our lives. Boundaries are essential for balancing productivity and order in the world. Think what Dallas, Texas, would be like if we had no signs to allow us to go certain speeds and no traffic lights to tell us when to stop or when to go. *Chaos* is a word that describes how affected our lives would be with no laws, rules, or regulations. Boundaries help keep us safe. When safe boundaries are violated, abuse happens, whether it is personal, spiritual, or professional. There are guidelines of nature, cultures, professions, and religions. These are formed by customs, habits, and language.

Boundaries are a way of saying yes or no and define your personal right to protect yourself and those you care about. Boundaries protect and guide.

Boundaries are signs, signals, indicators or borders of freedom. These signs are like a road map to tell you where you are going. They protect you so that you can make good choices in the way you live, love, relate to others, and, yes, give and trust.

The first step—and, I believe, the most important—in setting your boundaries is to know who you are and how special you are, thereby validating the need to protect yourself and others. Without boundaries, there is no order.

In my family there are certain traditions and customs that have evolved over the years to help set boundaries for my children that will carry over into adulthood. Here are some examples:

- Appropriate dress: How do we dress for home? How do we dress for going out to school or church?

- Sunday time: Schedule church, dinner at home, nap, and family time.

- Holiday customs: Christmas Eve, we attend church. Christmas Day, we celebrate with a holiday brunch, stockings, and, around 5:00 P.M., Christmas dinner.

- Proper behavior: What do we accept as proper behavior—courtesy, manners, speaking to others? This begins with family respect.

- Communication: Talk and communicate effectively to each other as family members and to others. Table talking—no one leaves the table until all are finished.

- Habits of cleanliness: What standards are there in our home as to when the beds are changed? What is done with dirty clothes or wet towels? Who does the laundry and who cleans the kitchen?

When the children were growing up, we set rules or boundaries for our home. Since I have used the bumblebee as a teaching tool and tried to be as positive as possible, I used it in our home and made our rules positive. (By the way, these have become a *Mama's Rules* book.)

- *Bee* kind and considerate to one another.

- *Bee* sure to brush your teeth—A.M. and P.M.—and floss daily.

- *Bee* clean and neat—pick up your clothes and keep your room clean.

- *Bee* willing to cooperate and *bee* courteous to all, including family.

- *Bee* at home by 10:00 P.M. each weeknight and 12:00 midnight on Friday and Saturday.

- *Bee* considerate of all family members by asking permission to bring friends home.

- *Bee* sure to use good table manners, including the proper use of napkins, silver, coffee cup, and glassware.

- *Bee* sure you plan what to wear and get it ready the night before a school night and set your alarm. (At age eight each of my children received an alarm clock for his or her very own use. At age twelve, each one received an ironing board and an iron and became responsible for ironing his or her own clothes.)

On the home front, setting boundaries is essential, and in the professional arena, it's just as important to establish and maintain certain boundaries:

- Be there on time. Leave home by a designated time (always early, never late).

Boundaries define what we want, need, think and feel.

- Be accountable by checking in and out.

- Stick to the allotted time for breaks and lunch.

- Limit personal telephone calls. The adage "a day's work for a day's pay" is about being honest.

- Use your computer for work-related tasks only. Also, use office equipment and supplies for business purposes only.

- Be aware of confidentiality. Keep business and your personal life confidential.

- Dress properly. (Be sure your attire is not a sexual distraction at work.) Be professional.

- Give others plenty of space. Respect their personal boundaries.

There are many generic areas of boundaries that are common in everyday life:

- what and when to eat

- zip codes and area codes

- musical scores

- fresh air

- dental needs

- pain tolerance

There are flexible and inflexible areas of boundaries, such as personal ethics, food, and morality. Perhaps you need to stop and redefine your boundaries and learn to be wise in surrendering your personal control to others.

We need to begin building our families to be honest, responsible, caring, hard working, and courteous. We need to convey hope for the future in a spiritual context—even in times of stress in our national arena. Our only hope is through God.

Twenty-five years ago, when I originally took Zig Ziglar's book to teach my students in high school, we could not mention the term *character education.*

The instruction was based on honesty, integrity, trust, and love, and I added responsibility and commitment. We were specifically told *not* to say we taught character—it was taboo. Recently I was on the same program with our national Secretary of Education, who now says we need to teach children to behave and act properly. I said, "Amen!"

Boundaries are the rules that set limits on our relationships. You've heard people say "I draw the line" or "Give me some space" or "Back off!" We all need to respect other people's limits, and we need them to respect our own. Everyone has a boundary system. We can tell when something's not right or when someone is getting a little too close. Boundaries define what we want, need, think, and feel. They set safe limits of protection. We get into trouble when we don't know our own personal limits. We often don't know when to say no. We get into trouble when we don't let others know when their behavior has crossed the line and offends us, as in sexual or verbal abuse

We can't control what others do, say, think, feel, or believe. But neither do we have to be the victim of someone else's messed up or perverted lifestyle. Recently, I visited my son Brian and his wife, Jennifer Mae, for a weekend. Brian took me to the airport in Baltimore at a very busy time. As he was driving, he tried to move over to the curb so I could check luggage, and a big passenger bus would not allow him into the right lane. In fact, the driver moved closer to my son's car and angled to try to break his side mirror off. Rather than getting upset or angry, my son responded by simply moving over and completely away from the bus. Oh, he could have had a very unpleasant collision, but Brian decided a long time ago not to allow someone else's anger to control or affect his decisions.

Building Boundaries

When you set limits or boundaries on relationships, others aren't as likely to take advantage of you, and your life will be a lot simpler and easier. It's hard to say why, but some people often try to change the other people involved in their relationships—more than likely to meet their own personal needs. You may not have power over what others do, but you *do* have power over what *you* do. It is a decision to set standards or boundaries. The earlier you set boundaries in your personal, professional, and spiritual life, the earlier you can control any situation.

Sometimes you may have to detach or distance yourself from an unhealthy relationship. That means separating yourself from another person's responsibilities and problems. Setting boundaries helps you disconnect from unhealthy people and become more independent. You begin to make decisions for your own good, and you stop being responsible for someone else's happiness. Friends who are constantly pulling you down are what I call "high maintenance." I personally do not have that much time for a friend like that. I have too many things to do.

Sometimes people may not be aware of how close they can get to you or when to back off on personal questions. It's your responsibility to let them know right away—in a kind but firm way. My usual comeback when someone wants to get too close with a question is to ask, "Why do you want to know that?"

You cannot let what someone else thinks about you affect how you feel about yourself, even though all of us need others' blessings, love, and care. (Believe it or not, there are personality differences.) You don't have to change who you are for anyone else, and you shouldn't be trying to change any other person. Remember, different is not wrong—it is simply different. You have the right to set standards and limits in your life.

You have the right to confront unacceptable behavior and to say no when you don't want to participate in something. I often say that *no* is a complete sentence. We need to put this into effect in our lives as well as teach it to our children. I believe this will help deter child abuse and greatly curb spousal abuse. You don't have to depend on anyone else for happiness and self-worth, so do not allow anyone to steal that from you.

Don't be an easy target for someone else to use or abuse. You need to be able to love yourself even when others don't. You need to believe that your life has meaning and purpose even when others don't believe that. If you respect yourself, others will respect you. It has to begin with you and flow out from there.

Boundaries help you untangle yourself from unhealthy relationships until true healing sets in. If people have been overstepping your boundaries, you need to limit their access to you. If someone is abusing you, using you, manipulating you, or controlling you, find out how he or she is controlling you and seek ways to prevent their control. If you can't seem to muster the strength to do this yourself, you may need to get professional help. If you set limits and the person steps over those limits over and over again, it's time to put some distance between that person and you. In my experience, if a person won't allow you to set limits and doesn't consider your needs, maybe he or she has a personal agenda of manipulation and control in mind rather than your welfare.

Boundaries work both ways. We also have to remember not to cross the boundaries of others. Without boundaries, we will be victims or offenders or both. We need to be careful about whom we allow into our personal space and to what degree. It's your responsibility to respect yourself and the rights of others.

Keep your boundary system intact with each relationship—spouse, parents, and friends—not allowing anyone to control your life. I personally believe that as you set healthy boundaries in your life, with Father God's help, you will gain order and peace as well as a good direction for life.

When my children were young, I was made aware of the need for physical, mental, and spiritual boundaries. We purchased a home, and the survey showed, in detail, a plot where the physical part of my property was. The fences on each side were indicators of the width of my lot. The front was the sidewalk, and the back was the creek. These were expressions of where my private property began and ended. To me, boundaries are indicators of where to go and how far.

Sometimes we are taught to be too sweet and docile, and perhaps we become the brunt of a cruel and mean individual. We need boundaries—or perhaps we call them rules—for both our personal and professional life. The areas need to be clearly defined, such as verbal, spiritual, relationships, and physical. This way we decide early on in our development to know "our space."

Family, friends, and colleagues should be aware of how we decide to live. "It seems to have taken a lifetime to understand that I do not have to understand everything about myself or others," my good friend Barbara Hammond stated, quoting her mentor, Mary Crowley.

Boundaries could be called principles of ownership. They add structure to our lives. Boundaries define life by saying who we are, who we will give time and energy to, where we are going, and what we care about.

One of the things people often ask me, knowing that I speak in churches, is "Do you believe the whole Bible?" And I say, "Yes, I do believe the whole Bible." As my friend and mentor Zig Ziglar used to say, "I believe it from index to maps." I tell my audiences that I'm not smart enough to know what to believe and not to believe, so I just believe the entire thing. In the Old Testament, there is a lot to learn, and the book of Nehemiah has always been one of my favorites, because I have led a life of rebuilding, as Nehemiah had it laid on his heart that his job was to rebuild the walls of Jerusalem. When God told him to rebuild the walls, he was actually a cupbearer, and he had no experience in building walls, but he felt they needed to be rebuilt so the people would be able to return to their homes and live in safety.

No sooner had Nehemiah and his people begun to rebuild the walls, than their enemies tried to intimidate them and stop them. Does this sound familiar? When you've tried to rebuild a part of your life—whether it's a marriage, a friendship, or the relationship with your children—people say, "There's no use in that. That's not going to work." And we let them intimidate us. Sometimes we're victimized by threats, ridicule, and lies of other people, and of course it discourages us. But when we are firmly committed to something, as Nehemiah was, we can see the project through, standing strong through its completion.

Many times we feel that God wants us to do certain things—rebuild a relationship, start a new job, renew a friendship, or apologize—and then people say, "Hey, you can't do that. You know it won't work." But when we know that it's the right thing to do, we can carry it through, no matter what others say.

Nehemiah knew that once the walls were rebuilt or restored, the people could rebuild the temple, but it would be a challenge. The walls would be their safety net, because as you know, they did not have safety alarms, screens, or double windows. This gave the people of Jerusalem hope.

The Bible says a man who lacks self-control is like a city whose walls are broken down. Our personal boundaries determine what we will and what we will not allow in our lives. Their established presence allows recovery to progress unhindered. In other words, when we make a firm commitment, saying we *will* do this, it's like what my mama said when she was left with nine children under the age of seventeen, and the family wanted to separate us—she said, "Ain't nobody goin' nowhere." Mama's statement is as colorful as it is profound. She took a firm stand to say *this is my family, these are my children, and we will make it.* And make it we did, even though I'm sure there were days of hunger, doubt, and discouragement.

This is how we decide how we'll live our lives—whether we're healing from relationships, addictions, or whatever. Please don't think that those boundaries cannot be restored once they have been broken down, because they can. We can always begin again. We can come back and enforce those boundaries again. If we don't, we haven't much hope of recovery from whatever our situation. We have to learn what to resist and to keep outside forces from manipulating us and talking us into doing something we know is not right. The lesson we learn here is that just as Nehemiah rebuilt the walls of Jerusalem, we, too, must build and set our own boundaries and enforce them so that our growth, whether spiritually or mentally, can go forward. We have to know where we're going from this point on in order to set good boundaries.

A boundary is an invisible protection that fits around one's personal God-given space. Boundaries keep people from abusing us, bursting into our space, and controlling us or getting us to do things before we have a chance to think and say no. You see, we each make the decision to say what and where our boundaries are and that no one can go past them. Our boundaries keep us aware of others' boundaries so that we do not break into their spaces to abuse or control them. These invisible fences mark off space around us just as parking spaces do in a parking lot. People cannot come into our spaces without our permission. We can build healthy boundaries around us by which we choose not to feel pushed down. It's not so much keeping people out as it is protecting ourselves from being controlled by others or controlling them. Setting boundaries makes for healthy relationships in a family, in a school, in a church, or in a business.

You can start right now on a journey to building your boundaries. No matter what age you are or what you've been through, you can start right now by saying "I want to rebuild." You're not disgraced for the rest of your life. You're not shamed for the rest of your life. You're not guilty. If you believe that you have been forgiven through the blood of Jesus Christ, you can turn your life around and realize, *Hey, here are some things I can do to set some boundaries and begin to enjoy life—even small things.* You can't do everything, but you can do something. I love what Mother Teresa said, "We cannot feed five thousand, but we can feed one." You see, whatever it is in our life that needs changing, we can always do something. S-T-A-R-T.

Our boundaries, principles, structures, and life mission should all be compatible. We should walk the talk. The degree to which we value life is evident in how we care for ourselves. If we feel valued, we take better care of ourselves, just as we would take good care of a valued item.

Several years ago, my husband's mother gave us a two-seater couch. I looked at the sofa and thought, *I do not have a place for a small beige couch.* I placed it in a spare room where it was out of sight and out of mind. I knew we needed to keep it because of the sentimentality of its being my mother-in-law's. Several years later, I wanted one of my bedrooms painted and chose khaki and light cream colors. A friend casually mentioned that the couch was beautiful and that it was upholstered in raw silk. It's amazing how I instantly treasured this couch when I discovered it was of value. This is actually a good analogy of how we should value ourselves when we realize we are children of the King. Our Father owns all the cattle on the hillside, and he has made us in His own image. Psalm 139 says we are wonderfully made. We only need to be reminded of our heritage in Jesus Christ.

Habits of people who don't set boundaries include:

- unkept promises
- overcommitment—cannot say no
- addiction to alcohol, drugs
- dishonesty and gross exaggerations
- neglecting health
- habitual complaining

- no respect for self

- out of control in life's situations

- two-faced—not realizing facts

If we do not have good boundaries, we often open our lives to weak friendships and relationships. We are prone to allow people to "suck our life blood" causing us to be vulnerable and controlled, tired and exhausted mentally.

In the highway of life we come across bumps, detours, and bad weather. The road signs are valuable in helping us know how fast to drive, when to slow down, and, yes, even when detours are necessary—just as on the shoreline of the ocean, there are posted signs warning us of undercurrents and deep water.

May I ask you a question? Would you be upset if there were a big sign—BRIDGE OUT—and it directed you around a would-be tragedy? I don't think so. So when your close friends or colleagues point out a detour for your good, you might want to consider the alternatives to proceeding. Slow down and read the signs. Each of us needs to encourage and be a good enough friend to give someone else caution. This might save you a lot of hurt, confusion, and disappointment.

Are you willing to self-evaluate?

When we are physically sick, we go to a medical doctor for an evaluation of our blood, iron, and so forth. We may very well be suffering from malnutrition in our bodies, which has made us ill. In the same way, we can become malnourished in the spirit. We need to evaluate our minds, thoughts, and beliefs according to the correct boundaries.

When a person is depressed or out of control, I often ask that person three questions:

1. Who are you spending time with?

2. What are you reading?

3. What are you watching?

Your answers to these questions are indicators of how you are affected daily by those you spend time with, what you read, and what you watch.

Keep a daily score. With 1 being the lowest and 10 the highest, circle how you feel:

Physically: 1 2 3 4 5 6 7 8 9 10

Mentally: 1 2 3 4 5 6 7 8 9 10

Spiritually: 1 2 3 4 5 6 7 8 9 10

Chapter 10

Confrontation and Communication

When one of my children came to me, telling me about inappropriate behavior by a person she loved and respected, my first thought was to shoot him, but that didn't last long. I knew that was not the answer, but it was my first response. I took the three children (ages nine, ten, and twelve) out to get a hamburger, and I told them that in our lives, sometimes people make inappropriate decisions or choices. I told them that a decision was made that was inappropriate, and I explained it to my children the best I could. Then I said, "I just want you all to know that this will never happen again." Brian, of course, at first, felt very, very angry. He was the man of the family so to speak—the male—and I'll never forget that little child saying how angry he was that anyone would hurt his sister. He promised, "I'll never let anyone ever hurt my family again." I told the children that we wouldn't make any quick decisions, but that I was going to talk to this particular person with the idea of confronting and being sure my children were safe.

I went back and talked to this person, and, as I tried to explain the problem, the person walked away from me. I waited awhile, and then I went back to the person and said we must talk about this. Again, the person walked away from me. Have you ever had a moment in your life when you felt that it was only you and God—and then He makes Himself known? That day, God gave me the peace and comfort I needed to keep from falling apart. It was a defining moment in my life. I prayed and thought about what to do. I called one of my sisters and told her what had happened, asking her to "just help me walk through this." She offered to come help me in whatever way she could. (I've always appreciated having an understanding family.)

I later decided I needed to confront the man and his wife. According to Jesus' instructions found in Matthew 18:15–17, when we confront someone, we need to talk to that person first. Then, if they don't respond, we should get a witness. If they still will not cooperate, we take the matter before the church authorities (when appropriate). If they refuse to cooperate, we may have to cut off contact with the person or persons.

My sister Evelyn, who is now deceased, did go with me. We sat down with the couple at the table and told them what my child had reported to me. The man never denied it. The woman expressed more anger with me than he did and said it was certainly a serious accusation. I told them what my child had reported to me about what had repeatedly happened. I told them that I believed her and that I was disappointed and confused. At that point, I let them know that they would never again have private access to my children. This was one of those times that you hope never happens, and I hope and pray that you who are reading this book will never have to do this. But we have to make tough decisions to protect ourselves and our children. In fact, if someone has abused your child or you know of a child who is being abused, the law now requires that you report it to the authorities. Please, please—listen, believe, and take up for these little ones.

When the doctor handed me my first child, Patti, I felt a love for her and for my husband that was new to me. It was a strong unconditional love, a passion. I felt this with each one of my children. I quickly realized this passion could work in reverse if anyone ever threatened or harmed my children. I made a commitment at that time to do whatever I could to watch out for and protect my children.

When adults spoke or acted inappropriately around my children, I needed to address it. I'm not sorry that I confronted this couple. I sat many, many hours with my children talking about the situation around the table. Naturally, I had to get advice. I got advice from a very dear minister, Dr. Harvey Saunders. I then called a mental health clinic—a very popular Christian one here in Dallas—and I told them the situation, letting them know that we needed family and individual counseling. As a family and as individuals, we received some of the best advice and counseling available. One of my children went to counseling for about a year. I believe that God gave me the wisdom to handle the situation—and the words and intestinal fortitude to do something about it.

If there is any one thing that I want to get across to you in this chapter, it's that if there is any inappropriate behavior of any kind—drugs or alcohol, or verbal, physical or sexual abuse—please look at the situation and take action. Don't just sit and think, *Well that's unfortunate*, and don't ever, ever accuse the children or make them feel it is their fault. As parents of these children, we have a responsibility to protect them. We need to listen to them, believe them, and take action. We won't always know what to do, but we need to do something. This is one of the reasons I put the SOS (Systems of Support) in the back of this book. Please ask for help. There is wisdom in the counsel of many, but we have to ask.

When we hear the word *confront*, we naturally think of friction or discord. However, the word means "to stand, to come in front of" or "to meet face to face." It also means "to acknowledge and to present both sides of a fact or problem."

In the case of abuse, the abuser is a manipulator who usually intimidates, demeans, and belittles the smaller or weaker person.

The manipulator in a home, business, or church or in social circles uses his power, words, actions, and even his threats to have others do what he wants.

My personal experiences in confronting have been successful only in the past few years, because I learned an effective way to confront—first, to organize my thoughts, and second, to choose the time and place. In the past, I did not know how to prepare for confronting or *negotiation,* as we call it in the business arena. As Chester Karrass states in his advertisements, "We get what we negotiate. We do not get what we deserve."

Time, thought, well-planned preparation, and prayer are the most important aspects toward a meeting of the minds in personal, professional, or spiritual life.

Someone said, "We fear what we do not understand." That is why confronting a bully or a controller is so important. No one deserves to live in fear of another person's actions or words.

There are several reasons we may be afraid to confront. We may fear rejection or the reaction of the individual, or we may be afraid we will not be able to define our feelings or that we will be disappointed. But the way we communicate will help us effectively confront. Some effective phrases to use when you approach the person are

- Would you help me understand why this happened?

- Is there any reason why we cannot meet to discuss some thoughts or concerns?

- I need your input or advice.

When you are preparing for a confrontation, be sure to write down your concerns, and choose the time, location, and time allotted. It's important for you to stay calm and to check your language, your tone of voice, and your body language. Introduce one concern at a time. Write responses down—document them. Be unemotional, and do not cry. Crying causes you to lose some of your control.

Think about what results you expect or anticipate. When you've said what you have to say, stop. When you ask the other person to explain, never interrupt. You may want to ask him to repeat the concern if there is a lot of emotion.

When the time is right, you may find it healing to confront the perpetrator in a way that suits your feelings and your situation. For instance, you might build new boundaries in a current relationship with a family member who abused you in the past. Communicate to that person that while you are working to heal from the sexual or physical abuse you suffered at his or her hand as a child, that you will need to take time away from him for a while—or perhaps for a lifetime. Reconciliation is not a requirement of forgiveness. You may even suggest that he attend a series of therapy sessions.

You might write a letter that you may not want to mail. Take as long as you need to write a letter to your abuser. Say whatever you need to say or want to say in the letter. Don't hold back. Express to the person exactly what you know he or she did to you and how it made you feel. You might talk about how the abuse has affected your life and how you feel about it now. Putting your feelings on paper may help you process how you respond or react to the feelings.

Whatever method you choose to assist in your healing, your action shows that you have acknowledged the harm done to you and that you are now willing to stand up and say that you will no longer take the abuse—no matter whether physical, verbal, or emotional.

You need to decide ahead of time that the response from the perpetrator is not your goal. You shouldn't expect the person to fall down at your feet and ask forgiveness. Even though you think he should, many times, he does not. More than likely, you will meet with opposition, denial, resistance, or even hostility. The triumph comes instead from your standing up for yourself and from placing the blame and the shame where it belonged all the time—on the perpetrator. Then realize that many have been where you've been, and decide what you can do to help others. Please care enough to confront.

In order to confront others in family, business, or other relationships, you need to create a feeling of open and caring lines of communication. That is why a plan of action as described in this chapter is vital.

Listen

Communication is an exchange of ideas and information using talk, gestures, writing, and body language. It is looking, listening, and feeling. Words alone cannot express our full intentions. Facial expressions, tone of voice, body language, and many other nonverbal skills are all a part of communicating with others. Those who have studied communication styles and patterns have concluded that two-thirds of the intent of a message is nonverbal. This leaves only one-third of the message to be communicated through words. We all have different communication styles, the most important being the spoken word, which either encourages or discourages. The Bible says in Proverbs 18:21 that death and life are in the power of the tongue. My advice is to speak with love and truth, encouragement and forgiveness.

Communication failures are stumbling blocks to good living, personally and professionally. We hear examples of them every day: "I didn't mean to say that." "She misunderstood me." "He lied." The result? The damage to human feelings, to business, to property and finances, even to international relations, is inestimable. We can avoid all this by communicating clearly, honestly, and effectively.

Strangely enough, I have found that the secret of being heard—of how to really talk to another person—is, for the most part simply to listen. Listen. Following are nine sound communication guidelines:

1. Listen with an inner ear. Hear what is actually meant, rather than what is said with words and with body language. Listening to the person talking helps to provide the emotional

support to solve the speaker's problems. Saying something out loud sometimes creates a clear understanding of the problem for the speaker and the listener.

2. Listen to the concerns of others. Don't concentrate solely on your own feelings.

3. Be sensitive to when it is better simply to listen and not offer advice, as with adult children.

4. Assume nothing. Allow the person to feel comfortable and to explain with talking.

5. Say what you mean. When you listen, respond. As Mama used to say, "Make your words tender because later you may have to eat them."

6. Before speaking, always ask yourself: What is the message that's needed?

7. Remember that communication is in the present.

8. Do not bring up what happened or mistakes he or she made in the past.

9. Listen with a gentle heart, and allow him or her to finish.

What you hear should be kept in confidence. There was a time I went to a person in confidence and later found out they had discussed it with their entire staff. I have never gone back to that "trusted" person again. This was a humiliation and additional hurt I did not deserve. Be a friend that others can trust.

Remember,
whatever comes from the heart
will reach the heart.

According to a leading business magazine, 90 percent of us clash with other people in our daily lives because we have trouble communicating effectively. We can avoid so many pitfalls when we communicate clearly, honestly, and effectively. The secret of being heard is simply to learn to listen. If we'll stop, look, and listen, we'll avoid collisions in communications.

The following guidelines on listening to young people are taken from an article written by Becky Wilson, a then tenth-grade student in a talented and gifted English class at James Madison Memorial High School. These are excellent thoughts for us to focus on when talking with our family, adult children, students, or grandchildren:

How to talk so we want to listen!

- Remember that we're adults…sort of…and don't need to be talked down to.

- Be honest with us. Sooner or later, we will find out the truth, and it makes us feel dumb if we were lied to. Besides, if we know the truth, we can help instead of becoming part of the problem.

- Tell us you love us—even if we act like we don't want to hear it. A hug or a pat on the back is always a nice bonus.

- Praise us if we do OK. Sometimes it seems like nothing we do is enough.

- Skip the lectures, please. A word or two and a check to see if we understand the message usually does the trick. Most of us know we've made a mistake long before you talk to us about it anyway.

- Don't yell! Nothing makes us want to fight back more than being screamed or shouted at.

- When we need help, give it to us—OK? We don't need to be told that we really blew it this time, that you would never have made that sort of mistake, or that our siblings would never have done it. We need help in finding our way out of the mess, not a lecture that we're in trouble. We already know that part.

- Don't pressure us to achieve all the time. We do our best, but we also get tired. Remind us from time to time to slow down, goof off, do something silly. We can't always make the goals you've set for us, because some of them are too far off the ground.

- Let us know that you'll love us even if we don't live up to your expectations. Let us know that you'll always be there for us, no matter what.

- If we do have a major problem, help us solve it, don't solve it for us, or we'll never learn how to function as adults.

- Let us form our own opinions about some things. Chances are they'll be a lot like yours if you've brought us up right.

- If we've got a collective problem, hear us out first before assuming you're right and we're wrong.

- Give us a chance to disagree with you without telling us that we're "talking back." We need to develop that part of our communication system, too.

- If you're angry, mad, sad, or whatever, tell us so we don't say or do the wrong thing. We know how it can be, and the last thing we want to do is make the situation worse.

- Don't bring up the same issue over and over again. Getting told off once is usually enough. We aren't all ego. There is common sense and logic there, too!

- We love to hear about when we were little, and we like to hear about your teenage years as well. But don't use those stories just to teach us a lesson or make a point about how good we have it. The stories are fun just by themselves.

- Never stop talking to us. You are the only ones we can count on for reassurance and love. (Families in Education Web site, Wisconsin Department of Public Instruction, Madison, Wisconsin)

It has been said that we communicate in many ways. Often we do not take the energy, patience, time, and understanding to talk and listen to those closest to us. Our words are often not well planned, and we demean and hurt without realizing the hurt caused.

There have been many times in my career that I felt inadequate, yet I remembered the kind words of those who had loved and encouraged me when I was a college freshman who needed validation.

As a thought for making others feel comfortable and less stressed, use laughter to lessen intensity of or nervousness about a situation. I believe laughter is a universal language and is the best internal jogging a person can experience. None of us needs a complete overhaul, but some of us may need just a little tune up to help us be aware enough to listen to, care about, and help others.

Chapter 11

Single Parenting

I recently went into one of my favorite restaurants here in Dallas—Houston's Restaurant. It was 3:00 on Friday afternoon, and I was hungry. I dropped in and was greeted very cordially by the hostess. I said to her, "Just one," and her reply to me was, "One is enough." This kind statement was a revelation to me about single parenting. One perhaps is all there is, and that is enough, but that doesn't mean it is easy.

A feeling of disbelief and shock settled over me as I witnessed my husband, at age forty-six, take his last breath. He died of a heart attack on September 26, 1981, while we were out of town on a business trip, leaving me a single parent of three small children.

My dream world of having a good Christian husband, a home, and children was shattered that evening. The one big goal in my life—to have a happy family made up of a mother, a father, and children—was gone in an instant. But because of God's way of healing our broken hearts, I've discovered that one *is* enough. In some families, one parent can be all a child has.

For those of us who are traditional, we plan to grow up, marry, and have children. We don't think about being single parents through divorce, death of a spouse, or an unplanned pregnancy. Yet those things happen every day. I realize that death of a spouse can be less painful than divorce or abandonment for all parties. You don't have to face rejection, gossip, or misunderstandings as much. But it is still painful, and there is grieving involved in all these situations.

The grief process is basically the same in serious matters of the heart. The first is disbelief or denial, and then come the emotions of anger or resentment, bargaining, and depression. The question, "What am I going to do?" rings in your head—then there's acceptance, and finally, a plan of action.

Our attitude toward divorce or being widowed can be a positive one or it can be a constant negative reminder of the end of the family unit as we knew it or wanted it to be. It entirely changes our physical, mental, and spiritual life. We can either become bitter or better. It's our choice. The difference is only one letter—the letter i—but it carries powerful ramifications.

The changes one experiences due to the death of a spouse or divorce are both hurtful and a great loss; however, though accepting of the hurt, processing the anger, and getting help, healing can take place.

Hurt never leaves us where it found us. We will be different, and things will change, but do understand things can become better. I chose to believe the best is yet to be. This gave me hope in the midst of loneliness and despair. The good part of raising children as a single parent is that God has given me a special relationship with my children, for which I am grateful. It is a bond that I feel will never be broken.

We as single parents need to understand that it is impossible to do all that two people had previously accomplished together. Single parents are often overwhelmed to the extent of total exhaustion, irritability, loneliness, and depression, not to mention depleted by the financial challenges of only one paycheck.

But when children are involved, we must be sure of our attitude concerning our family, realizing we have the total responsibility of their education and of their emotional, spiritual, physical, and financial well-being. I have noticed that some women talk incessantly about their "broken" homes. It begins every conversation. This is a fact, and repeating the fact will not change it, but it can negatively affect one's attitude.

I feel that positive words are the best way to address home, family, and friends. Being positive is an attitude that children feel daily—and it helps validate their worth. Every divorce or separation does not have to be *The War of the Roses*. We need to keep in mind the family as a whole and to deal with each problem as it arises, understanding that a done deal is a done deal. In other words, "The boat sank. Let's get over it."

Even in the case of losing a spouse through death, there are still many unanswered questions that arise frequently. I remember coming in from work tired, with supper to cook, clothes to wash, dishes to wash, and so on. As we sat down to eat, one of the children became angry because I could not attend all of her functions. She had only me to express her hurt and anger toward. I took that moment to look her in the eye and say, "Do not be mad at me. I'm here. I haven't left you. I do all I can, and that will have to be acceptable enough." Of course, angry statements from our children hurt us and sometimes place false guilt on us, but this is only temporary.

I found that sitting down with my children each night to eat dinner together was important, so the rule was that nobody left the table until everyone was finished. As a result, they began to talk and express thoughts, concerns, and issues of the day. This rule became a habit that still exists today when we are all home for a meal. We remain at the table until all are finished. Certainly I didn't do everything right as a single parent, but this habit has definitely been rewarding.

Please, please, please listen to your children and grandchildren. Children should be loved, believed, and accepted. It is important. Try to create an atmosphere of trust and confidence. Many times, children have no one to love them, listen to them, and care for them. Children expect support and compassion in cases of hurt or mistreatment by family and friends.

The home is where teaching responsibility begins, and it overflows into every area of our adult life. No one person need take all the workload of a home. Learn to delegate according to the age of the child, but be sure each family member has weekly responsibilities.

When my children were small, I decided to write down each one's weekly chores to be accomplished by noon on Saturday. These lists were placed on the kitchen counter by Thursday evening. They could do their assigned tasks on Thursday, Friday, or Saturday morning. However, if they wanted to sleep in on Saturday, they made sure their responsibilities were done by Friday evening. I used a checklist for the children to complete. As jobs were completed, they were marked off the list.

One thing I discovered as a single parent was that I had to hang on to my sense of humor. I have a special never-married single friend, Dr. Mary Allen, who says that she is an unclaimed blessing. She would rather "want something she did not have than have something she did not want." (I personally believe the entire atmosphere of a home can be changed with humor.) The country-and-western song puts it another way: "It's sad to belong to someone else when the right one comes along."

If you're single or have become single again and you have children, you're on a new journey as a single parent, and the end of the story has yet to be written. Maybe you did not choose to take this route, but here you are. I am encouraging you to take some steps forward on your journey rather than continuing to make the same wrong choices and having to start over again and again. Sometimes, we continue to shoot ourselves in the foot. Whatever you are faced with, your life is not over—in fact, you've just begun a new chapter. Maybe you've had questions in your mind about what to do next and how to do it.

Walk the Talk

Through my own experience and input from other single parents, I've come up with a list of helpful hints. It is important for a child to recognize the family values because it establishes unity and order. Values are taught and caught.

A dozen bees to build a strong family unit

1. *Bee* willing to accept and value yourself and family members: children, spouse, parents, and grandparents.

2. *Bee* consistent, honest, firm, and fair in all rules and values.

3. *Bee* open about showing affection—hugging, kissing, sharing, and listening.

4. *Bee* a good example. Children will do what we *do* more than do what we *say*.

5. *Bee* genuinely interested in each other's lives and daily activities.

6. *Bee* pleasant to each other. Show respect and good manners.

7. *Bee* willing to allow your children to suffer their consequences (i.e., they pay for their own traffic ticket). Allow them to fight their own daily challenges.

8. *Bee* creative in sharing household chores. Delegate.

9. *Bee* patient. Praise in public, and discipline in private. I feel that it is an embarrassment to all when you correct others in public, whether it is your spouse or your children.

10. *Bee* honest, ethical, moral, and true. Live as you should, based on biblical principles.

11. *Bee* willing to be the parent—not a tyrant or a friend. Take leadership in family matters. Take leadership financially, too.

12. *Bee* a spiritual leader. Allow your entire family to be aware of tithing, giving to missions, and supporting others in church and family. Walk the talk. Show the same love, courtesy, and good attitude on a daily basis as you do on Sunday or in public.

The process is as important as the product

When the children's father died in 1981, the children were five, six, and eight. The need to feel whole again after his death was very important to me. I realized that it would take lots of time, effort, tears, friends, and prayers to work toward my feeling that we all were a unit again. I discovered on this part of my journey some practical steps to take to reestablish (or to establish for the first time) a strong family unit.

First of all, we need to change our methods and terminology. We should talk as a family unit, taking time to discuss what is happening with our children and family. Healing for the family will come more easily if we do not call attention to negative terms that sometimes have a perception of less-than, terms such as *divorced* or *single parent*.

I think we all agree that staying positive is hard. We can't expect to change our lives if we listen to only one tape, read one book, or listen to one speech. It's an ongoing growth process. I heard my mentor Zig Ziglar explain it this way: I took a bath yesterday, and I had to take another one today. Just because you have to do it every day does not mean it is not effective. We need to understand that "being positive" is a decision we must practice daily.

As you read good, positive books, underline and mark phrases and sentences that are meaningful to you and yours. Consider using different colored markers to designate phrases, words, and stories; then when you pick up the books later, you can readily identify passages that are important to you.

Get organized. Write things down. I am a firm believer in letting paper remember so you can forget. Of course, now instead of paper and pencil you may allow your Palm Pilot or computer to remember for you. Just putting something down somewhere for later visualization is important. Many of the suggestions given involve making lists. You will find this an invaluable tool.

I suggest you have a good positive Christian tape or CD in your car at all times while you are running errands or traveling. It has been said that you have to hear something for twenty-one days for it to become a habit. Pick up good habits by listening to inspirational tapes or CDs, music, and speeches.

Adopt a symbol. I choose to wear the bumblebee when speaking to remind me to *bee* the best I can be every day. I mentioned in chapter 2 that the bumblebee can be an inspiration to each of us because it does what is supposedly impossible, that is, it can fly despite its heavy weight and light wings. But the idea of taking inspiration from the bee is not new. The Egyptians used a bee to represent perseverance and hard work. Napoleon's officers wore a bee on their uniforms as a symbol of courage. Today, many athletic teams wear a bee on their uniforms to symbolize their ability to overcome the impossible.

The I Can label is also effective for changing old attitudes. When I was a high-school teacher, I realized how many times students said "I can't." The words *I can't* were being used much too frequently, I told the students, "You are always saying, 'Prove it to me.' As a business teacher, I have to prove debits and credits. I want you to prove to me that there is such a thing as an 'I can't.' I want you to tell me the size, shape, and color of an 'I can't.' " You can imagine the responses I received. "Oh, Mrs. McCullough, that's impossible!" they said. "All right," I told them, "I want you to bring a tin can to class tomorrow." I didn't tell them what shape or size or kind to bring. That night, I cut out pictures of eyes from magazines.

The next day, there were thirty-two students with thirty-two different sizes of tin cans. Some had Vienna sausage cans, some had soup cans, and some had gallon peach cans. Some of the boys had dragged the huge trash cans in from around the campus, but each of the thirty-two students had a tin can. The individuality of each of the class members really stood out. As I looked at the group, I was graphically reminded that each person is an individual who deserves to be treated with respect.

The students could hardly wait to see what I was going to do with those tin cans. I gave each one of them one of the pictures of an eye I had cut from the magazines and told them to paste the eyes onto their cans. "When you put an eye on a can, what do you have?" I asked. "You have an 'eye can.' When you say it, the words come out 'I can.' You can see, touch, and hold it, and you can describe this 'I can' to someone else." This idea changed the students' attitudes and served as a reminder that "I Can. You Can, Too!"

The I Can way of life has a foundation of character, honesty, loyalty, integrity, trust and love. You can readily see there is no easy way to success. But the combination of positive attitude, good self-image, good relationships, goal setting, strong desire, and willingness to work leads to a much more fulfilling life as a single parent.

Something else you can do to encourage yourself is to make a victory list. Our victories and our mistakes are either steppingstones or stumbling blocks. List all the positives in your life. You will find they far outweigh the negatives.

Look for the good in others. An ounce of gold is covered by tons of dirt, but we don't look for the dirt—we look for the gold. Find the gold in people. Practice seeing people as they *should* be and not as they *are*. Think of someone who has had a positive influence on your life or someone you consider to be your hero. Write that person a note and talk about the influence he or she has had on you.

Start something new (making new friends, a hobby, a new career, a book, etc.). Do it now. When you don't know how to do something, start. Start now. Be a person of action.

Practice random acts of kindness. Do things for others with no selfish motive—just do these things out of the goodness of your heart. Smile and speak to strangers. Send appreciation notes and even flowers. Pick up the tab for a less fortunate stranger at a restaurant. These random acts of kindness don't have to cost a lot of money. Just help others to know that they are special and important.

Being a single parent doesn't have to be the end of your dreams. It can be a new start for you—and for your children. Make a dream list. This is a list of things you would like to achieve assuming there are no obstacles to prevent you from achieving them. Think about some of the things you want to be, do, and have in the tomorrows of your life. Once you begin thinking about your hopes, dreams, and visions, it is important that you begin believing you can have or accomplish them. Some people call this *imaging,* that is, *seeing the reaching* in your own mind. As we begin to believe and see the reaching, we begin to achieve. If you don't have dreams, you will never have hope of seeing a dream develop into reality.

Instead of making a list, you might choose to make a do-be-and-have collage. Find attractive pictures in magazines that illustrate your desires. Cut out these pictures, slogans, words, and phrases and glue them on poster board. Place the collage on the wall in your room so you will be reminded of what you want to be, do, and have. Think it, see it, believe it, expect it, and achieve it. You and your kids can even do this together.

Set goals. Identify your goals, state them positively, state them as if they were fact, and state them in objectively measurable terms.

- List the personal benefits you expect to gain from achieving your goals.

- What are the major obstacles?

- Identify the skills or knowledge required to reach your goals.

- Identify the individuals, groups, companies, and organizations to work with to reach your goals.

- Set completion dates.

Every action is a

value statement

I suggest you set goals in seven areas for a balanced life—(1) physical, (2) mental, (3) spiritual, (4) family, (5) financial, (6) career, and (7) social—and review them often. Goals are your road map to success. Many of your goals will overlap into several areas of your life. However, one of the keys to success is to prioritize. Work toward classifying your dreams into one of the seven areas. Finally, the difference between a goal and a dream is that a goal is simply a dream that you are willing to take action on.

A demonstration of goal setting is to select someone and give him or her a crushed piece of paper. Have him stand about five feet from a wastebasket with his back to the wastebasket. The idea is for him to try to hit the basket from that distance without seeing it. Then have the person face the wastebasket and try to hit it from a longer distance. Then move the person closer to the wastebasket and let him try again to hit it. The idea is that if we pursue a long-range goal that we cannot see, we are not likely to achieve it. If it is a long-range goal we can see, we are more likely to come close to succeeding. And if we take short-range goals we can see, we will systematically move closer to success and eventually achieve it. Write your personal definition of success. What must you invest to achieve it?

My definition of success is this: Doing your best today.

List ten of your friends and the quality or qualities you most admire about them. Then do a personal inventory to see if you find some of these same good qualities in yourself.

Show all people compassion, love, and patience. Little things can make a difference—a smile, a thank-you, and a nod are all encouragement for others. We all need to feel capable and appreciated. Remember the Golden Rule—"Do to others as you would have them do to you" (Luke 6:31 NIV).

Be aware of your influence. Determine what impact you want to have on your children and how you will go about it. Every action is a value statement.

Set your priorities—God, family, career—for a well-balanced life. Refer back to this list on a regular basis and determine if you are on course for achieving them. Remember the five *P's*: "Proper Planning Prevents Poor Performance." Organize and prepare for work and family. Strive for balance between the two. I feel that this is even more important in a family with only one parent.

Evaluate your lifestyle, and include family members to help with chores as well as with fun times. Make a list of chores to be completed daily by each family member. Set aside one night per week that is family night. Turn off the television and participate as a family in an activity—playing a game, working on a craft, performing a skit, or doing another fun activity.

William James, the father of American psychology, stated that the most important discovery of our time is that we can alter our lives by altering our attitudes. Define the words *attitude* and *aptitude*. Why is your attitude more important than your aptitude? How can you improve your attitude? Regardless of how good or how bad your attitude may be, you have the power to change. You cannot control the situations that occur in life, but you can control your attitude toward those situations.

We need to be constantly aware of the ways we can be more effective in getting along with people. The way we motivate others will determine our effectiveness in working with them. Whether working with business associates, teachers, our peers, or our family, we constantly have influence on others.

Plan to have a perfectly positive day. I realize many times we have perfectly negative days. Think about the last day you had when everything seemed to go wrong. Think of some of the things that went wrong (overslept, missed your ride, was late for school, had a headache, did poorly on a test, missed a sale,) Now think about the events that tend to lead to a perfectly positive day (got six to eight hours of restful sleep, had a good breakfast, was complimented by others, got an *A* on a test).

You are what you are because of what goes into your mind. You can improve what you are and where you are by improving what goes into your mind. Right thinking precedes a positive attitude, and a positive attitude leads to more perfectly positive days.

Lighten up. We need to look for ways to use humor in everyday situations. Nothing releases stress, physical or mental, as much as a good laugh or smile. Look for cartoons, music, comedy, stories, and people who can find humor quickly. Learn to laugh at yourself. A sign I recently saw read:

> I'm lost—I've gone to look for myself.
> If I should return before I get back,
> please ask me to wait.

Many years ago, a consultant offered one idea to a company owner to help the company's employees become more productive. The consultant challenged the company owner to use the idea for one month and then pay him whatever the owner thought was fair. Thirty days later, the consultant received a check for $35,000. This was a considerable amount of money to pay for a single idea. The idea the consultant gave the company owner was to have each employee write down the six most important things he or she had to do for the next day before they left work each day. A very simple idea—worth a great deal to anyone who will use it. When the children are all tucked into bed at night, you can take just a few minutes to make your Six Most Important Things list for the following day. Believe me—it saves time, energy, and worry. Along the same lines, keep a daily planner—there are many on the market today to help us become organized.

Sometimes we have to tell the truth in advance. Right now we may not feel enthusiastic or cheerful, but each time we verbalize those positive feelings we come a little closer to feeling that way. Keep this in mind: "Logic will not change an emotion, but action will." Begin telling the truth in advance on a regular basis to help maintain the right mental attitude. Say to yourself out loud, "I'm _____, and today I'm going to be (truth in advance) _____,

One of my strongest convictions is that you can make your life better—no matter how bad your situation is today.

I believe in you

No matter what you've done—*I believe in you.*

No matter what's happened to you—*I believe in you.*

No matter what people say—*I believe in you.*

No matter if you are rich or poor—*I believe in you.*

No matter your age, size, or IQ—*I believe in you.*

No matter where you live—*I believe in you.*

No matter your position or lack of one—*I believe in you.*

No matter, no matter, no matter—*I believe in you.*

You can use this poem to address someone who needs encouragement to let them know that "no matter, no matter, no matter," you believe in her. You will find that it is a powerful tool.

Give yourself permission to succeed in all areas of your life. Make a commitment to excellence to becoming more healthy in relationships, more professional in business, more successful in parenting, and so forth (example: I, Mamie McCullough, give myself permission to succeed in *writing this book.* My commitment *will help other women to recover from hurts, abuse, and life's disappointments*).

I Can, and here's how you can, too:

- *Bee* there. Bloom where you're planted. Have the courage to persevere in the face of adversity.

- Discover your mission and purpose in life.

- Become a person of love and discipline. "Work hard. Stay clean. Love others. Go to church. Forgive others." These are still words to grow by.

- Remember that your perspective makes the difference in life. The way you look at life is your reality. My mother could have looked at what she didn't have and given up. Instead, she looked at what she had, and life got better every day.

- Look for the lessons in life, and be willing to learn. Your victories and your mistakes are either stepping stones or stumbling blocks. You determine which by your willingness to learn.

In our world of fake diamonds and faux furs and digital image manipulations, we wonder if what we see, hear, and know is actually real or bogus. The world has always needed real people. Each one of us needs to be valued by others. Be a person of value. Be real. Being real means accepting your past as experience and having hope for the future.

Encouragement

Here are some things to say to encourage your children:

- You do a good job of... (find what they do well).

- You have improved in... (find small things to compliment).

- I love you, but I do not like what you do... (criticize the performance and not the performer.

- You are important to me and I value your feelings.

- I value your opinion.

- Let's try to work this out together.

- So you made a mistake. What can you learn from your mistake?

- Keep trying—don't give up.

- I'm sure you can do this job, but if you need me, you know where to find me.

- I understand how you feel, but I know you can handle it.

- You are a valuable part of this family.

- I think you are special because…

- I love you just the way you are.

- People are more important than things.

What all children need

As a single parent, you can help your children have a good self-image and be successful when you apply the following truths:

Love. Children need to feel

- that their parents love, want and enjoy them.

- that they matter very much to someone.

- that there are people near them who care what happens to them.

Acceptance. Children need to believe

- that their parents like them for themselves just the way they are.

- that parents love them all the time, and not only when they act according to parents' ideas of the way children should act.

- that parents always accept them, even though often parents may not approve of the things they do,

- that parents will let them grow and develop in their own way.

Security. Children need to know

- that their home is a good safe place they can feel sure about.

- that their parent(s) will always be on hand, especially in times of crisis when they need them most.

- that they belong to a family or group—that there is a place where they fit in.

Protection. Children need to feel

- that their parents will keep them safe from harm.

- that parents will help them when they must face strange, unknown and frightening situations.

Independence. Children need to know

- that their parents want them to grow up and that their parents encourage them to try new things.

- that parents have confidence in them and in their ability to do things for themselves and by themselves.

Some of the ideas that I felt were helpful to my children after my husband's death were these:

- A picture of their father in each child's room

- Always talked about father's birthday and parents' anniversary

- Listened to music in lieu of TV

- Took time to grieve

- Kept in touch with his family

- Remembered the good times we had, such as going to the zoo and on trips.

- Took time to express feelings—listening at the dinner table

To those who have a friend or family member who has become single again, I urge you to be a little more sensitive to their needs. They still need to be loved and accepted. I encourage you to reach out and invite them to dinner, have them over for a cup of tea, or pick them up for church or a community function.

We cannot control what others think or believe, but we must keep a check on our attitude to make sure we do not become calloused and hardhearted. When my husband, Don, died, to help keep my heart soft and forgiving, I wrote my feelings down in a letter.

Letter to my deceased husband— October 1981

Why did you die and leave me with all these problems? I do not know how to be a single parent. What am I going to do? I am confused! Do I stay here in Dallas or return home to Georgia to be by my family?

Don, how can I go on with the children to raise? How do I adjust? I am angry! Things were going so well, and then you left me.

How do I juggle school, groceries, church, athletics, and clothes for Patti, Brian, and Jennifer? Who will stay with the children while I travel? Oh, I wish I felt something different.

What do I do with taxes, lawn mowers, and being single again? I never intended to be single and have to raise the children alone. I am angry!

I wrote what I was feeling at the time, and as I gave it all over to God, the healing began. Even through the adversities, we grew into a strong family unit. We knew our Father God would take care of us, and He did.

The children gave me this plaque last Christmas, and I think it says it all.

WE ARE A FAMILY

Since before any of us were born, God planned for us to share our lives with each other. He knew exactly how our strengths and weaknesses would balance one another, and the depth of love, understanding, and commitment we would learn to feel. He knew the richness of our separate characters would be developed through the hard times, and that mutual trust and respect would be born as a result of overcoming the trials together. He knew we needed each other...to hug, to help, to teach, to serve...to love.

Gail C. Copeland

A perfect day of joy—making memories

Some of you may wonder about my life as a single parent. I am pleased to report that God has allowed me many days of joy. I believe we all should imagine what a perfect day of joy would be and then strive as often as possible to fulfill this vision. Just to show you how it's done, I want to share with you what my own perfect day of joy with my children has been like over the years.

I planned my joy day around Saturdays so that everyone would be home. I rose early, put on my jogging outfit, went outside, and jogged for half an hour. I am not a happy jogger. I run for my health. I jog alone and never worry about my safety. If you saw what I looked like when I first got out of bed, you would know why. Phyllis Diller and I are probably the only two women who can jog in a park and lower the crime rate.

After my jogging, I would come back and read for half an hour or more as I cooled down. I am still committed to a program of continual study. Mark Twain once noted, "The man who can read but doesn't is no better off than the man who can't read." I read for fun and for study. I like the idea of beginning each day by making myself a little wiser than I was the day before.

After reading, I bathed and got dressed. I put on my makeup and fixed my hair. If the milkman or mailman came to my door, I was presentable. If neighbors or relatives or business associates came by unexpectedly, I was ready. My motto, which I mentioned earlier, is Get up, make up, dress up. I've always tried to look as nice on Saturday for my children as I did during the week for other people. I do not mean I was dressed in professional clothes. However, being clean, having makeup on, looking good, and having a good attitude were important to me.

Once I was dressed and ready for the day, I worked until noon. I handled the household chores that stacked up during the week and took care of any organizing work that needed to be done to prepare for my travel during the coming week.

After lunch with the family, I usually would take a short nap. The rest of the day, I spent with my children. We went to the zoo, played Monopoly, took a walk, toured a museum, visited some good friends, or just sat on the porch swing and talked. We really didn't care, just so long as we were together.

Some of the most precious times my children have to remember are those activities we did on Saturday afternoons. One summer Saturday afternoon, we decided to make mud pies. We lived—and I still do—on a creek where there is a lot to do, so we always had a yard full of children. That Saturday, we had eight kids over at our place. I asked them, "Do y'all want to make mud pies?"

"Yes, yes," they cried.

"All right, we'll make mud pies. You decorate them and I'll judge them and give ribbons for first, second, and third place." They were excited about doing that. They went out and made mud pies and decorated them. In the meantime, I went into the house and cut three blue ribbons, three red ribbons, and two yellow ribbons—eight ribbons for eight kids.

I went outside, and there they were, proudly standing before their pies. "Patti," I said, "you get a blue ribbon. Jennifer, you get a blue one, and Brian, you get a blue one." Naturally, those were my three children getting first prizes.

One little boy asked, "Why did you give them first prize? That isn't fair!"

"What do you mean, 'It's not fair'?" I asked him.

He retorted, "It's not fair. You're their mother, and you gave them first prize."

I looked at him and said, "Son, if you want to win first prize, you get your mama over here to judge."

Now, folks, that child didn't speak to me for several months, but I feel that the one place a child should always win first prize is in his own yard. If you cannot be first place in your own yard, where can you be? Unconditional love is needed in every home, school, and community in our nation. No one needs judgment as much as unconditional love. We will not like everything our children, spouses, or the people with whom we work do, but we still need to love them.

I remember thinking, *Years from now, when my children and I are sitting around the Thanksgiving table, someone is going to laugh and say, "Mama, remember the time we made mud pies and you let the three of us win first prize?" Then we'll all roar with laughter about the memory we made in 1985.*

Life can be very good. It's just all in what you make of what happens to you. Some seventeen years later, my three are all grown up in their twenties and are married to wonderful mates. Patti and Matt Wyman live here in Dallas and have one son. Thomas. Brian and Jennifer Mae were married in 2001, and live in Baltimore, Maryland.

My youngest daughter, Jennifer, married Scott Kruba here in Dallas in the summer of 2002. The children have reminisced about the memory of the blue ribbon mud pies many times—and laughed at how upset their neighborhood friends were. But they know I love them unconditionally. That is a done deal. I made the decision to love them, even if I do not like all they say and do. I pray this one memory will be handed down to my grandchildren, family, and friends.

Chapter 12

Surviving Cancer

It was June 1, 1999. My last child had graduated from college, and I was beginning to see the light at the end of the tunnel for the first time in twenty years. And for almost four of those years, I'd had three children—Patti, Jennifer, and Brian—in college. This is what we laughingly called "mal-tuition." As a widowed single parent, I almost felt a freedom. It was only three weeks later, however, that I found out I had breast cancer.

I finished my treadmill walk and took a shower. When towel drying, I realized something was wrong with my left breast. I was over fifty-five. (I tell people that I am exactly 59.95 plus tax—and tax keeps going up.) I was physically active. There was no history of breast cancer in my family. Within hours, however, I had met with my general physician, had numerous sonograms and mammograms, and had seen a breast surgeon—all to be told I needed a radical mastectomy immediately—the following Monday. Even with the shock of the news, I remained intact. I was emotional, of course. I cried, but I felt a peace, knowing that God had everything under control. I had given my heart to Him at an early age and had studied the Bible, sung the wonderful hymns of faith, and trusted Him. Now I was standing on His promises.

Still, I was uneasy and emotional about the future. Telling my children was the most difficult. They were shocked and upset as I told them I had breast cancer and would need a radical mastectomy. I had a level 3 malignant neoplasm of the breast. I choked back the tears as I saw the hurt in my children's eyes because of the seriousness of the surgery. I was fortunate, though, to have my primary physician recommend Dr. Sally Knox at Baylor Hospital in Dallas, Texas.

The morning of the surgery, my family and I got up early and prayed together around my kitchen table before going down to Baylor. I felt the Holy Spirit of comfort and peace so strongly. When we arrived at the hospital, many family members and special friends were in the waiting room praying for me, and I felt the presence of the God of Peace.

When Dr. Knox sat on the side of my table before surgery, she asked, "Are there any questions?" I answered, "No." So she asked if she could pray with me. "Yes!" During her prayer, I drifted into a land of nothing. I remember a nurse named Judy calling my name and praying for me. This is how I awoke from surgery.

Then the one night when I was in the hospital, my good friends Dr. and Mrs. Kenneth Cooper came by to visit. Dr. Cooper encouraged me to begin exercising my arm immediately. The next day as I was leaving the hospital, Dr. Knox also encouraged me to place my hands together and lift them over my head ten times each hour while I was awake—beginning immediately.

Needless to say, I was sore, bandaged, two drains out of my left breast area, depressed, and felt as if every part of my body was being separated. But—I knew I had to try. "I can do all things through Christ," and I kept that promise on my lips. I cried, grunted, and groaned, but I was determined to come back as well as I could, and I knew it would take faith and action—including a consistent program of exercise.

Taking action is not always easy, but it's necessary to take back our mental, emotional, and physical health. As a result of doing what I did not feel like doing and did not want to do—for four weeks—I can truthfully say I have 95 percent range and feeling back in my arm.

I learned some life-changing principles through this cancer:

- Turn it all over to God—for peace, understanding, and recovery.

- Be willing and obedient to those professionals or experts—in other words, listen. For me, the experts were Dr. Sally Knox and Dr. Ken Cooper.

- Take action. If we do what we need to do when sometimes it hurts the worst, we can recover. I did, and you can, too.

- Keep an attitude of gratitude toward those who have researched and helped you.

- Decide how you can help repay those people.

I volunteered to speak at the Susan G. Komen Survivor Luncheon. We may not be able to directly repay those who help us, but we can pass it on to someone else. I will continue to help and encourage those who have just been informed they have cancer and those who are cancer survivors. God takes our hurt hearts and turns them into healed helpers.

What can we do to help combat this disease? Here are some suggestions:

1. Begin to exercise regularly. Exercise reduces risks. Stay active.

2. Eat well—fruits and vegetables, fresh-fresh-fresh foods. Write down everything you eat.

3. Avoid or limit coffee or caffeine.

4. Never neglect checkups.

5. Get yearly mammograms after age fifty.

6. Keep your attitude positive. Look for the best—handle the rest.

7. Read—read—read. Fill your mind with good materials that encourage you and give you hope. Personally, I think the Bible is the most positive book ever written.

8. Get adequate rest. Of course, the amount of sleep required varies from person to person.

9. Plan special fun activities with family and friends.

I believe it is not what happens to you, but what you do with what happens to you that matters. The exciting news that brings so much hope is that in the 1990s, the death rate from breast cancer declined the largest amount in more than sixty-five years, and it is continuing to decline. I made the decision to continue to work and enjoy life as much as possible. I did nothing to cause cancer and could do nothing to stop it. Life has an interesting way of pulling us back to the reality of what we value and love. Family and friends are so important, and their encouragement and unconditional love is priceless.

The good that came from this cancer was the fact that I now have the opportunity to speak to people in cancer seminars throughout the country. On June 8, 2002, I celebrated my three years of surviving cancer—with a greater hope than ever before.

Don't ask why but ask instead,
What can I do to help make things better?

Chapter 13

Forgiven, but Rarely Forgotten

I was visiting some friends recently, and while we were catching up on years gone by, I asked about some people I had known years ago. The friends asked me why I had asked about how this couple was doing. I simply said they had taught me a lot of good things earlier in my life and I would always be grateful to them. My friends quickly replied, "Mamie, don't you remember how they talked about you after your divorce and how badly they hurt you?" I said, "Yes, I remember, but I decided long ago that forgiveness was about me—not the people who hurt me." Biblically, we are to forgive seventy times seven. Forgiving is an act of obedience and is God's way of equipping. From this experience, I've learned that there are those who can hurt us temporarily, but not permanently. They may not change, but we can.

The perfect example of forgiveness is the parable of the Prodigal Son found in Luke 15:11–32. A successful man had two sons. One requested his part of the family inheritance before the time of his father's death. He left home and squandered his inheritance, ending up destitute and starving. When he returned home to ask if he could just be one of his father's servants, he felt unworthy of forgiveness.

His father met him with open arms, gave him a robe to wear, and placed a ring on his finger. The young man's father was filled with compassion toward his son; the father was thankful to have him back home. The older brother, because he had not been disobedient and selfish and had remained home to work alongside his father, was angry and resentful when he heard that his father had forgiven his younger brother.

Do we celebrate enough when our brother falls and comes back? Or do we judge and condemn? The Bible says we should forgive seventy times seven. The way the father forgave his wayward son is a perfect example of how we should forgive.

> *My father sexually abused me as a child, but I have never told anyone. I felt I could not say anything out of fear that I would hurt my mother. My greatest pain is that I love my dad very much and I wish I could tell him I forgive him.*
> *—Anonymous*

We all know we're supposed to forgive one another, but it's not that simple to do. Forgiveness isn't making allowances or forgetting what was done. It isn't an open door for more wrongdoing, and it isn't necessarily reconciliation. It is breaking the power of pain, anger, and hatred. When someone hurts us, it's in our power to forgive, whether that person ever acknowledges the harm or ever apologizes. Naturally we want an apology, but we may never have that kind of closure. When we choose to forgive, we not only express the power we have, but we also break the power the wrongdoer had over us. We're saying, "I release you from the guilt, and I will no longer be manipulated by the memory of this or the emotions it evokes." When we try to get even, the cycle of hurt never ends. When we forgive, we begin the healing cycle and the hurt lessens. We'll never forget; however, we need to stop focusing on the pain. We also need to forgive ourselves. Whether we have been carrying around a burden

If you seek
revenge, you dig
two graves.

of real or false guilt, forgiveness will lighten the load and allow us to continue in the healing process.

> *It's time to let go of a lot of my past. I went through a "wild" time after high school, and God has forgiven me, but I haven't forgiven myself and "gotten on with my life." Please pray for me.*
> —*Cheryl*

When we truly look at our lives, forgive ourselves, and allow God to shape us, then sorrow, guilt, remorse, fear, shame, jealousy, pride, envy, and hate no longer have their hold on us. We become free to love ourselves as God loves us and free to live for Him.

If there is someone who has hurt me, I make every effort to begin to forgive him and practice blessing him. For instance, if this person is critical, I affirm to myself that he or she is loving and full of praise. If they are grouchy, I affirm that they are cheerful and fun to be around. If they are cruel, I affirm that they are gentle and compassionate.

God never loves us more or less. He loves us unconditionally, and that is what I try to do with those around me, even those who have hurt me. Believe me, it's not any easier for me than it is for you, but with God's help, I am learning. This is a concept we *all* find hard to grasp, but forgiveness is more about the one offended than the offender. I have finally realized that forgiving is not an emotion. Forgiveness is an act of the will.

———•———

It's important for us to forgive those who have wronged us, whether they are family members, church friends, coworkers, or neighbors. This is a painful process, but is one we have to work through in order to be free from their control. Hurt is often more about power than destruction. True forgiveness comes when you think of those who hurt you, and you can wish them well.

Forgiveness is *not*

- understanding the offender's point of view.

- forgetting.

- condoning.

- controlling.

- taking on the role of a martyr.

Forgiveness *is*

- celebrating the most incredible mystery of God's work in our life.

- a sign of positive self-esteem.

- letting go of our grudges, resentments, hatred, and self-pity.

- part of an ongoing healing process.

- giving up the need for punishment.

- freeing up and putting to better use the energy once consumed by holding grudges, harboring resentments, and nursing unhealed wounds.

- moving on.

God has given us His most precious gift to forgive—His grace. Through Jesus, God gives us grace to love, enjoy, and forgive others as well as ourselves. In the process of forgiveness, we travel through phases or steps in a cycle: pain, uncontrolled emotions, decision to heal, knowledge, expression, and restoration. Then, as time passes, we realize the hate is gone, the revenge is gone, and the hurt is gone. The hate, revenge, and hurt are only a memory, and we are going on with our lives to take what happened to us and use that knowledge to help others.

Here are some thoughts to consider when in the process of forgiving:

- You do not have to like the person who hurt you.

- You do not have to be around the person who hurt you.

- Remember that God has paid for sin. He loves us just the same way before and after abuse, hurt, or rejection.

> Be kind and compassionate to one another,
> forgiving each other,
> just as in Christ God forgave you.
> Ephesians 4:32 NIV

Unforgiveness is the desire to keep punishing the other person. If anyone else is responsible, such as a parent, forgive also the one who allowed the abuse. If you can do this and forgive yourself, you can begin the healing.

- Amnesia is not a prelude to forgiveness. Forgiving empowers us to move beyond the hurt.

- Recall times when you've been forgiven for your faults. Those recollections may help you to be more forgiving of others.

- Separate the wrongdoer from his or her deed. Doing so will help you to see the deeper truth about the person—that he or she is a weak, needy, and fallible human being, just like each of us.

- Realize that if you cannot free people from their wrongs and see them as the needy people they are, you enslave yourself to your painful past and make your future bleak.

- If you're in a position to confront the wrongdoer, do so without attacking the person, but with the full force of your honesty.

Your goal is to be able to say, "What you did hurt me. I forgive you—and I will make every effort not to let you hurt me again."

- Some relationships can be mended with forgiveness; others are beyond repair, and the most you can seek is civility and the ability to wish each other well.

Forgiveness is a choice. The question isn't, "*Can* you forgive those who have hurt you?" but "*Will* you forgive them?" Turning loose of the hurt is the beginning of healing.

These factors help determine your capacity to forgive:

- *Critical background.* If you came from a critical, harsh upbringing where you were faulted for a lot of things, you're likely to grow up to become self-critical as well as critical and unforgiving of others.

- *Temperament.* Sensitive people are going to be hurt more often, so the issue of forgiveness will be harder to tackle. More stoic, easygoing people are harder to hurt and have fewer occasions to practice forgiveness.

- *Faith.* Religious faith plays an important role in the ability to forgive. This is the basis of all forgiveness. A spiritual base helps provide you with unexplainable wisdom and strength.

Forgiveness is not only good for the soul, but it is essential for good health. When we stew in a lot of hatred, we can be affected by sleep and appetite disturbances, high blood pressure, ulcers, headaches, skin rashes, and fatigue. It can affect our productivity at work, our concentration, and our ability to get along with our coworkers.

Many times, we would rather throw away a relationship with a family member or friend than to confront and work to resolve the resentment. We tend to think it would be easier to replace the relationship than to repair it. Few of us can forget what happened, but we can forgive in order to deny anger and unforgiveness their power over our lives.

Certainly we need to be aware of daily forgiveness. One way I've found that helps me get better is celebrating National Forgiveness Day. I celebrate it every year on April 3 because that's my birthday—a day I will be sure to remember. Each year on National Forgiveness Day, I take a personal inventory, listing and taking time to forgive anyone that I may not have forgiven and to think about how I could ask for his or her forgiveness. Forgiveness is the best medicine to begin the healing process.

Forgiveness happens in four stages:

1. Hurt—when somebody causes you pain so deep and unfair that you cannot forget it.

2. Hate—when you cannot seem to shake the memory of how much you were hurt and you cannot wish your enemy well.

3. Healing—when you develop the ability to see the person who hurt you with new eyes, to see the person as a frail, fallible, human being.

4. Reconciliation—depending on the circumstances, and facing the wickedness of what was done to us, not excusing or ignoring the wrongdoing, but facing it, reconciliation can take place. Sometimes this stage will simply lead to civility and peace between the two parties.

If we can't free people from their wrongs, then we remain slaves of the past and let our hate become our future. In one way or another, we are all hurting. Even those who seem happy-go-lucky are hurting in some way. There are parents with a prodigal son or daughter, casualties of broken homes, abandoned spouses, persons who have suffered from the effects of disease, and, of course, victims of abuse.

> *My father was very verbally and physically abusive towards me throughout my childhood. He always told me, "You're dumb and ugly, but you do have personality." I had low self-esteem, and I truly believed that I was "dumb and ugly." I finally went to a therapist, and I realized I am NOT dumb and ugly. I feel like a new person. I am working on having a relationship with my father. I don't hate him anymore, and I am actually trying to forgive him.*
> —Brenda

Only God can shut down the waves of depression and feelings of loneliness and failure that come over us when we are hurt. Faith in God's love alone can salvage the hurt mind. The bruised and broken heart that suffers in silence can be healed only by a supernatural work of the Holy Spirit, and nothing short of divine intervention really works. God will step in and take over if we allow Him to. God comes forward as a loving Father and demonstrates that He is there, making things turn out for the good. There may not be a one-time, cure-all, solve-everything prayer, but God does provide a way of escape. When you hurt the most, it's a good idea to go to your prayer closet and weep out all your bitterness. Then begin to look up. Encourage yourself in the Lord. Relax in the arms of Jesus and simply trust Him.

Prayer of forgiveness

Hold up to the Lord all the things about the person that trouble you. It's important to verbally state each thing or write your thoughts in a journal. Pray:

> *Lord Jesus, I give You each one of these things and ask that You take them and pour Your love and healing power through them. Thank You, Lord, that You have the power*

and the grace to redeem them. I ask You, Lord Jesus, to lift all the pain and hurt that has been involved with each one of these things. Thank You for releasing this burden from me.

Forgiveness leads to recovery

As I have stated, the purpose of this book is not only to make others aware of the cruelty of abuse, but to give hope and healing and a foundation by which the abused can start to heal. Someone once wrote, "It's never too late to be what we ought to be." I challenge you today to begin taking at least one small step to freedom. Here are some steps each one of us can take to begin our walk toward wholeness:

1. Take a damage inventory. Take some time to think through and put your feelings about the incident(s) on paper.

2. Write a letter to the person or persons who have hurt you. Be as specific as possible. You may choose to throw the letter away.

3. Draw a map of the places of hurt—streets, houses, or rooms. Describe the sights, sounds, and smells when the abuse happened.

4. Revisit places of hurt with someone who loves you unconditionally—a family member, friend, or trusted counselor. This was very effective for me.

5. Confront the person, if possible.

6. Seek wise counsel from qualified professionals.

7. Have a quiet time with God. Get your spiritual life in order with daily Bible study and prayer.

8. Learn to avoid friends who are destructive. Stay away from negative thinking friends who pull you down and mentally dump "garbage" on you.

9. Learn to smile, laugh, and give yourself permission to "feel good." Laughter is the best internal jogger one can have.

10. Be a mentor to those who need to heal and recover. You can often learn more when you teach or mentor. Pass on the good, and stop the bad.

11. Stay in fellowship with other believers for healing and accountability.

12. Make a list of areas in which you could give of yourself. Some suggestions are

   • Missions—Become a part of a program to help home or foreign missions. In your neighborhood, deliver meals, help the elderly, or visit nursing homes or hospitals.

   • Homeless—In each community there are those less fortunate who need your help to be fed, clothed, or encouraged.

   • Children—Get involved in helping children in your local school, church, or community. Volunteer to be a mentor.

   • Women of abuse—Volunteer at a battered home. Collect items needed. Encourage the staff.

   • Elderly caretaker—Many elderly do not have family to help them.

   • Education—Help others to become aware of abuse.

   • Giving money—On your local level there are those very near who need your support. Have a systematic way—once a month, volunteering at a shelter, school, or such—of reaching out to those who have hurts, perhaps worse than yours. This is one of the best types of recovery therapy.

13. Have a personal improvement plan that involves physical exercise, healthy eating, plenty of sleep, and a quiet time.

Begin to rebuild your own self-image, working on improving your education and your outward appearance: hair, nails, feet, and clothes.

14. Learn to trust and forgive others—yes, those who have violated your trust: family, friends, teachers, and church leaders.

15. Your mental vision, dream, or goal keeps you filled with hope. I have discovered some intriguing characteristics of vision and leadership:

   • The vision begins with a person who has a picture or an idea firmly entrenched in his or her mind.

   • Through a continued growth process, the vision stretches, changes, challenges, improves, and begins to live in your life.

   • Soon the vision becomes a big picture of possibilities.

There are also steps to take in developing your personal vision. Begin by defining your vision. Then put a time limit on it. Know how to begin, and surround yourself with those who will hold you accountable. If you want your dreams to come true, you have to quit dreaming and start. Vision is the greatest leadership trait you can possess. Without a vision, the people perish.

You can count on it:
God is good, and He has a plan for your life.

Realize that Satan is behind all abuse. He is the father of discouragement. It is his best tool. Do not blame God. He is a God of peace, love, hope, and harmony. Open your heart—unlock the heart—and share. The old tapes keep sending signals that affect your relationships in marriage, finances, and other important arenas. The tapes continue, but you can replace them and choose the right thoughts about yourself. Be sure you go to a godly counselor who gives principles according to scripture. Do not allow any counselor to violate a scripture. Refuse to retaliate or to get even. Allow no revenge. Retaliation is never, never right. The best revenge is to live well. Be careful how you think—do not talk hurts daily.

It's important to face problems like depression, anger, fear, guilt, and poor self-esteem. Be aware of the tendency to shut off emotions, and try to allow the child within to express previously suppressed emotion. Establish that the perpetrator is 100 percent responsible and accountable, as well as any co-contributors. Remember, the victim is innocent—not guilty. Begin implementing practical steps to change. Read material that will provide knowledge, support, and encouragement. Acknowledge forgiveness. These steps are important to become all you were meant to be.

To keep my attitude straight, I say the following personal affirmations and have done so for the past few years. Sometimes this is only lip service, but it helps me continue to keep going. I promise myself

- to be so strong that nothing can disturb my peace of mind.

- to talk health, happiness, and prosperity to every person I meet.

- to make all my friends feel that they are important to me.

- to look at the sunny side of everything and make my optimism come true.

- to think only of the best, to work only for the best, and to expect only the best.

- to be just as enthusiastic about the success of others as I am about my own.

- to forget the mistakes of the past and press on to the greater achievements of the future.

- to wear a cheerful countenance at all times and to give everyone I meet a smile.

- to give so much time to the improvement of myself that I have no time to criticize others.

- to be too large for worry, too noble for anger, too strong for fear, and too happy to permit the pressure of trouble.

Affirm: Today is my day. Victory is near.

Father, I, _____, thank You for Your unconditional love for me. Thank You, God, for turning my shame into praise. I know I have failed, but I am not a failure. Thank You, God, for allowing me to let go of the past along with the shame, guilt, and confusion. Thank You, God, for allowing me to forgive those who have hurt me—to not let the past rob me of my relationships, joy, peace, self-worth, and productivity. Thank You, God, for helping me to stop the bad in my life.

Thank You, God, for Your Word. I know and believe what the Word says to me and about me. Today I, _____, confess that I am released from unforgiveness toward myself and others. Thank You for helping me to process my hurts. I will be obedient and trust You, God.

Chapter 14

Every Ending Has a Beginning

This entire book is from a layman's heart—*my* heart—and it is the culmination of a twenty-five-year desire to help others who have fallen victim to some of the most hurtful and devastating problems of life. My hope is that you can believe and understand that someone cares—that *I* care.

A couple of friends were walking along the beach near the end of the day, after a big storm had washed thousands of starfish up onto the shore. Knowing that the starfish could not survive outside the water, one of the men reached down, picked up a starfish, and carefully returned it to the ocean. His friend asked him, "Why bother with that one starfish? What difference does it make?" The man, without pausing, replied to his friend, "It matters to that one." If you are the only one who finds help in the pages of this book, it's worth it to me. God cares about *you*, and so do I.

Perhaps this can be your time to surrender all your hurts, disappointments, and unhappiness to God and begin your life of health and peace. It's your decision to ask God for help and to make yourself available for the blessings He has planned for you.

While working on writing one of my other books, I was convinced that the information I was sharing with my readers could make a difference. Had I been on trial for my life, I could not have been more open or honest in my efforts to say to you, *If I Can, You Can Too!*

To be convicted of murder in the first degree, the law requires at least three things: The first is proof there was a murder, which usually means finding a body. The second is proof that the accused actually did the deed. The third is proof of intent.

To be convicted of caring and of encouraging in the first degree, the law would require at least three things. First, proof that someone actually does care about others and encourages them, which usually means finding a well-adjusted, joyful person who is cared for and has been encouraged. Second, proof that the accused actually did the deed. Third, proof of intent.

Please allow me to submit the following evidence. In the first place, there are people who live hopeless lives. These people are stuck in a rut. And as you may know, a rut is nothing in the world but a grave with the ends kicked out. These "walking zombies" began life with hopes, dreams, plans, and the desire to make a difference in the lives of others. After living for years with little or no care or encouragement, they have to make a conscious effort simply to be able to put one foot in front of the other. Their attitude, will, or spirit is being or has already been murdered—drowned in the ocean of life's hurts and problems. Someone must help them move from the storms of life to the safety of the shore.

Based on your letters, and the kind words you share when we meet in person, my books, tapes, and presentations are encouraging you and those you care about to seek the more abundant life (which is available to all of us). Many of you are actual eyewitnesses to the exciting sight of a life turned around. So I confess my intent. With God's grace and blessing, more than anything in the world, I want to encourage YOU to be all that God meant you to be and to have all that God meant for you to have when He placed you on this planet.

God bless you and keep moving!

And what about you?

Whatever God asks you to be, He will enable you to be. God will fix your broken heart, but you have to give him all the pieces. He will give you life and hope. As promised in Psalm 147:3, "God heals the brokenhearted and binds up their wounds" (NIV).

You and I have completed the first part of our journey of hope and healing as we walked through the pages of this book together. Our roller-coaster ride has now come to an end. I hope you have gained some insight that you can use to continue on your journey even long after you've read the last page of this book. I'm glad you made the decision to come along.

The story is told of the university president who loved the pomp and pageantry of graduation. He took special pride in welcoming the parents and guests, introducing the guest speaker, and handing each student his diploma. As the newly degreed men and women walked across the stage, our hero would loudly call out a hearty "Congratulations!" and clasp the hand of each and every graduate. As he did so, he would lean forward and whisper a personal thought without ever causing the diploma bearers to break stride.

One of the proud parents couldn't help noticing the president's enthusiasm and eagerly waited until she could get to her daughter after the ceremony to find out what personal wish had been bestowed.

After hugging her daughter, she asked, "What did Dr. Smith say to you as he handed you your diploma?" Her daughter smiled and replied, "He whispered, 'God bless you' and 'Keep moving'!" And the truth is he would have been hard pressed to give better advice to these young men and women. Certainly his wisdom was shown in helping keep the ceremonies from dragging on as graduations are prone to, but in addition to that, there was great wisdom in his comments for the long-term future of each person. If we are to enjoy this life and make the most of it, we must "keep moving."

When you pass through the
waters, I will be with you; and
when you pass through the
rivers, they will not sweep over
you.... For I am the Lord your
God, the Holy One of Israel,
your Savior.

Isaiah 43:2–3 NIV

We should never allow the bumps, valleys, or mountains to keep us from believing in ourselves and others. Things may slow us down or there may be detours, but we must always remember that God is good, all the time—and, all the time, God is good.

Years ago, I was drowning in a sea of hopelessness, and God, along with my friends and family, helped me make it to shore. After I made it to shore, I stood on the shore and watched you wave and plea for help, not knowing what to do. I believe that God has finally allowed me to complete this book and extend it to you as a lifesaver to help *you* make it to the shore as well. Now, you can dry off and crawl up into that safe place, as we smell the fresh-starched dress and fresh-cut grass—and listen to the whippoorwill's chant. I hope you have found your safe place, full of comfort, peace, healing, and love.

I believe in you. I always *have* and I always *will*—but I want you to remember more than anything else that *God* believes in you, too. He always *has*, and He always *will*.

SOS—Systems of Support

Following is a list of helpful hotline numbers, addresses, and information:

How to report suspected child maltreatment

If you suspect a child is being maltreated, or if you are a child who is being maltreated, call the Childhelp USA National Child Abuse Hotline at 1-800-4-A-CHILD (1-800-422-4453). This hotline is available twenty-four hours a day, seven days a week. It can tell you where to get help and how.

(From the National Clearinghouse on Child Abuse and Neglect Information Web site, nccanch@calib.com)

Specific agencies will be designated to receive and investigate reports of suspected child abuse and neglect. Usually, this will be carried out by Child Protective Services, the Department of Human Resources, or the Division of Family and Children Services. Police departments in some states may also receive reports of child abuse and neglect.

Following is a list of states' toll-free telephone numbers for reporting suspected child abuse. This number can be called within the state only. For states not listed, or when reporting cases from another state, please call the national hotline number in the box above. Web addresses are not available, but you may get more information at nccanch@calib.com.

Alaska (AK)
800-478-4444

Arizona (AZ)
888-SOS-CHILD
(888-767-2445)

Arkansas (AR)
800-482-5964

Connecticut (CT)
800-842-2288
800-624-5518 (TDD/hearing impaired)

Delaware (DE)
800-292-9582

Florida (FL)
800-96-ABUSE
(800-9622873)

Illinois (IL)
800-252-2873

Indiana (IN)
800-800-5556

Iowa (IA)
800-362-2178

Kansas (KS)
800-922-5330

Kentucky (KY)
800-752-6200

Maine (ME)
800-452-1999

Maryland (MD)
800-332-6347

Massachusetts (MA)
800-792-5200

Michigan (MI)
800-942-4357

Mississippi (MS)
800-222-8000

Missouri (MO)
800-392-3738

Montana (MT)
800-332-6100

Nebraska (NE)
800-652-1999

Nevada (NV)
800-992-5757

New Hampshire (NH)
800-894-5533

New Jersey (NJ)
800-792-8610
800-835-5510 (TDD/hearing impaired)

New Mexico (NM)
800-797-3260

New York (NY)
800-342-3720

North Carolina (NC)
(Contact the appropriate County Department of Social Services
for the number.)

North Dakota (ND)
800-245-3736

Oklahoma (OK)
800-522-3511

Oregon (OR)
800-854-3508, ext. 2402

Pennsylvania (PA)
800-932-0313

Rhode Island (RI)
800-RI-CHILD
(800-742-4453)

Texas (TX)
800-252-5400

Utah (UT)
800-678-9399

Virginia (VA)
800-552-7096

SOS—Systems of Support

Washington (WA)
800-562-5624

West Virginia (WV)
800-352-6513

Wyoming (WY)
800-457-3659

Agencies and addresses

Center for the Prevention of Sexual and Domestic Violence
   2400 N. 45th Street, #10
   Seattle, WA 98103
   206-634-1903

Chadwick Center for Children and Families
   Children's Hospital and Health Center
   3020 Children's Way MC 5017
   San Diego, CA 92123
   619-278-2365
   www.chsd.org

Childhelp USA/IOF Foresters National Child Abuse Hotline
   800-422-4453 (twenty-four-hour hotline and referrals to your
   area)

Department of Children & Youth Services
   Division of Community Programs
   Helping with emotionally disturbed children and young adults
   in need of independent living skills
   404-728-1567
   Fax: 404-982-9877

Domestic Violence Institute
   50 S. Steele Street
   Suite 850
   Denver, CO 80209
   303-322-0103

Family Support Services
 Amarillo, TX
 800-749-9026
 (outside of Amarillo)

Family Violence and Sexual Assault Institute
 6160 Cornerstone Court, East
 San Diego, CA 92121
 858-623-2777, extension 406
 www.fvsai.org

HOPE Counseling Services
 National Headquarters
 3418 Olsen Boulevard, Suite B
 Amarillo, TX 79109
 806-358-7000
 800-HOPE955

Incest Survivors Anonymous
 P.O. Box 5613
 Long Beach, CA 90805-0613

Justice for Children
 P.O. Box 42266, Dept. P
 Washington DC 20015

Military Family Resource Center (MFRC)
 1745 Jefferson Davis Highway
 CS4, Suite 302, Room 309
 Arlington, VA 22202-3424
 703-602-4964
 (DSN) 426-9053
 http://mfrc.calib.com

Mothers Against Sexual Abuse
  P.O. Box 2966
  Huntersville, NC 28070
  704-895-5964
  www.againstsexualabuse.org

National Center for Missing and Exploited Children
  Charles B. Wang International Children's Building
  699 Prince Street
  Alexandria, VA 22314-3175
  703-274-3900
  800-843-5678
  www.missingkids.com

National Children's Advocacy Center
  200 Westside Square, Suite 700
  Huntsville, AL 35801
  256-534-6883
  <www.ncac-hsv.org>

National Coalition Against Domestic Violence
  P.O. Box 18749
  Denver, CO 80218
  202-544-7358
  www.ncadv.org

National Committee to Prevent Child Abuse (NCPCA)
  332 S. Michigan Avenue, Suite 1600
  Chicago, IL 60604
  312-663-3520

National Council on Child Abuse and Family Violence
    1155 Connecticut Avenue, NW
    Suite 400
    Washington, DC 20036
    202-429-6695
    http://nccafv.org

National Council on Family Relations (NCFR)
    3989 Central Avenue, NE
    Suite 550
    Minneapolis, MN 5541-3921
    888-781-9348 763-381-9331
    www.ncfr.com

National Resource Center on Domestic Violence, Child Protection, and Custody
    National Council of Juvenile and Family Court Judges
    P.O. Box 8970
    Reno, NV 89507
    800-527-3223
    www.nationalcouncilfvd.org

Open Arms Home
    6250 NE Loop 820
    NRH, TX 76180
    817-281-1204
    www.openarmshome.org

Parents Anonymous of California
    (Prevents and treats child abuse)
    7120 Franklin Avenue
    Los Angeles, CA 90046
    213-875-0933
    800-352-0386 (in California)

Agencies and addresses

Safer Society Foundation, Inc.
P.O. Box 340
Brandon, VT 05733-0340
802-247-4233
www.safersociety.org

Survivors of Incest
P.O. Box 21817
Baltimore, MD 21222

U.S. Department of Health and Human Services
200 Independence Avenue SW
Washington, DC 20201

Sources

"Anxiety and Panic: Their Cause and Treatment." *Psychology Today*, April 1985.

Barron-Tieger Web site, www.personalitytype.com.

Cantrell, Mike. "Family Violence" in Commissioner's Report. *Dallas Morning News.*

Cloud, Henry, and John Townsend. *Boundaries.* Grand Rapids, Mich.: Zondervan Publishing House, 1992.

"Domestic Violence in the Family Hurts Us All." S.O.S. pamphlet, Southeastern Oklahoma Services for Abused Women.

Frank, Jan. *Ten Steps to Recovery*, 1983.

Gardner, John W. "Self-Renewal." *The Futurist*, November-December 1996.

Highfill, Pamela. *Cancel the Guilt Trip.*

"Hurt Ones, The." *First* magazine, 17 August 1992.

Roy, Jennifer Comes. "Silent Sadness." *Dallas Morning News*, 21 June 1999.

Rush, John. "Beating Depression." *Facts On File*. University of Texas Southwestern Medical Center.

"The Devil's Best Tool." Gospel Tract Society, Inc., P.O. Box 1118, Independence, MO 64051.

Toufexis, Anastasia, reported by Georgia Harbison. "The Lasting Wounds of Divorce." *Time*, 6 February 1989.

Vachss, Andrew. "You Carry the Cure in Your Own Heart." *Parade*, 28 August 1994.

Van Buren, Abigail. "Internal Causes of Anger." *The Anger in All of Us and How to Deal with It.*

Van Buren, Abigail. "15 Reasons to Leave Your Lover: Warning Signs of an Abusive Personality" in *Dear Abby*. *Dallas Morning News*, 18 January, 2000.

Walker, Lenore. "Cycle of Violence." *Florida Times-Union Shorelines*, 18 December 1993.

Ward, Henry Matthew. "Today" in *Dear Abby*: *Mobile Register,* 22 October, 1995, P.4-E.

Watson, Andrea. "When Words Hurt." *Lubbock Avalanche-Journal*, 25 August 2000.

"When Our Leaders Fall." *Virtue Magazine*, July-August 1987.

Wilson, Becky. "How to Talk So We Want to Listen!" *Families in Education Communication* booklet. Wisconsin Department of Public Instruction, Madison, Wisconsin.

Mamie speaks and conducts seminars for businesses, schools and churches. To schedule Mamie, call or write to her at:

Mamie McCullough
305 Spring Creek Village, PMB 372
Dallas, Texas 75248

1-(800) 225-4226
(972) 437-5308

Visit Mamie's web page for products, encouragement, and speaking information.

www.mamie.com

Other materials include:

Books: *I Can. You Can Too!*
           Get it Together and Remember Where you Put It
           Mama's Rules for Livin'
           Rules for Success